NURS
IN THE '60s
MY STORY

LIZ ALLPORT

APS Books,
The Stables, Field Lane
Aberford, West Yorkshire,
LS25 3AE

APS Books is a subsidiary of the APS Publications imprint

www.andrewsparke.com

INTRODUCTION

"You ought to write a book". I heard these words so many times, from friends, family, but most persuasively from hospital staff I met recently during three admissions to hospital and frequent out-patient visits.

They asked: "What's your occupation?"

I replied: "I was a nurse, but now…"

"Bet you've seen a few changes" usually came next and when I did reminisce, they were fascinated, genuinely interested, and told me I should write my memoirs.

So here a history of me. Everything I have written actually happened. Of course names have been changed to ensure confidentiality. I have written extensively about my first ward, mainly as this was my first experience of illness and death. Fortunately, the ward sister and staff nurses were kind and natural teachers. They laid the foundation for kind, empathetic nursing, attention to detail and team working.

Then there's happened over the next two years of our training and responsibilities as we gained experience.

We actually moved to several different hospitals during our training as the School covered The United Birmingham Hospitals, and I was fortunate to train in The Queen Elizabeth Hospital, Birmingham General Hospital, Birmingham Children's Hospital, The Women's Hospital and the Midland Nerve Hospital. I then successfully passed the State Registration Examination and worked as Staff Nurse and then Senior Staff Nurse in the Casualty Department at the General Hospital.

In 1970 I became Ward Sister on the men's surgical ward at Corbett Hospital, Stourbridge. After a break to have my children I returned to accident and emergency work at Birmingham Children's Hospital, followed by several years as Night Sister at the Queen

Elizabeth Hospital. This was where I became interested in teaching, making Further Education my main occupation until I retired. But that's a whole new story.

Liz Allport

Part I
1965-1966

A Dream

Midland Red. Top deck. Front seat.

We always sat there for a long journey. Mom didn't drive, but liked to have a full view of the road ahead. She linked her arm through mine and patted my knee. A quietly strong woman, Mom had lost her father in World War 1 and had spent World War 11 praying for news of her beloved husband's safety as he made his way across Europe after escaping from a prisoner of war camp in Italy. She was a strong formidable woman.

I'd dreamed of being a nurse since childhood, devouring novels like 'Jean Becomes a Nurse' by Yvonne Trewin and now I returned my completed application form to the Queen Elizabeth School of Nursing in Birmingham.

My invitation to attend for interview for the next intake in May, just six weeks away, requested a parent to attend the interview with the candidate. This threw Mom into a proper tizz; which dress to wear, buying new shoes, booking a shampoo and set the day before. I was happy in my black polo neck jumper, high boots and the red suit I had made myself.

"You know she's worried to death about going with you to the QE. It's not hospitals she's worried about - it's the fact that it's the QE. Everyone is in awe of that hospital. She's convinced she'll let you down," explained Dad. "All this shopping and stuff is just to hide her anxiety. She's never had an interview in her life."

I phoned the School of Nursing to assure them I was old enough to look after myself, receiving a frosty reply from a weary administrator: "A parent is requested to attend whenever possible". That had strong undertones of *I've heard it all before, so just get here and stop faffing about!*

Friends and family had some fun with this request. The most popular reason was to make sure my parents realised they may have to help keep me on nurses' low wages now I'd given up a well-paid office job.

Unfamiliar with Edgbaston, we had agreed we would stay on the bus into Birmingham. And then get a taxi out. This proved to be a good move. All the roads looked very similar, with the large Edgbaston houses. The taxi circled round, past the medical school and then we saw it. QEH looked magnificent, and suitably regal, in keeping with its worldwide reputation for ground breaking research and medical procedures. I'm sure the road was made to present the hospital at its best.

Red brick, with six floors of large windows each view making me more and more excited. Early morning sun reflected off large panes of glass forming the corners of the building.

The taxi stopped halfway down the drive. On our right were wide steps leading to the heavy front doors of the hospital, on our left a miniature version of the hospital, Nuffield House, the nurses' home.

Mom paid the driver and up the broad decorative stone steps we went. Two wooden-framed doors swung open and two sprightly, laughing nurses bustled out. My eyes followed them across the drive to the hospital entrance. Yellow dresses with white starched aprons over their arm, but most of all, the white, very starched, cap, folded into a neat triangle at the back. They were everything I longed to be.

Mom pulled me back to reality "C'mon love" she said quietly.

Steering me to the reception desk where my name was ticked off what looked like a very long list, the receptionist directed us to double doors with an ornate gold-lettered sign, *Ballroom*. Three girls and their mothers were sitting bolt upright on a row of chairs. Mothers clutched their handbags as only ladies of that age do, while one prospective nurse swung her crossed ankles backwards and forwards. I decided she had reverted to childhood, and so sat down as far away from her as possible. We nodded to each other and then at other interviewees and their mothers as they arrived. Not a word was spoken.

The stiff, uneasy silence was broken as a smiling secretary introduced herself as Miss Flynn and called "Louise Aldridge please". She led Louise and her mother away. The remaining mothers and daughters exchanged weak smiles.

Louise returned beaming; "It's not so bad - hope to see you all again" - and made her escape.

Miss Flynn reappeared and called my name. To this day I can't recall much of the interview. There were questions about my schoolwork (not my favourite topic). On my first day at school I had received an 'order mark' for walking on the wrong side of the corridor and seriously wondered if this petty attitude was going to work for me. However I must have managed sufficient 'O' and 'A' levels to confirm my ability to cope with the academic learning.

I remember assuring them that I was aware that nurse training included some unpleasant tasks, late shifts and night duty.

Mom went next.

"How did it go Mom what did they ask you?"

"They asked if I thought you would be a good nurse, so I told them: 'If Elizabeth sets her mind to something she can do anything, and do it well.'"

Love yer' Mom!

May 1965: Getting Started

The acceptance letter arrived with many precise instructions of what to pack into a trunk with my name stencilled on it in white capital letters. Thank goodness for the local Army and Navy store. Dad accompanied me as the store was a previously forbidden place. I don't know what he expected me to see. My school friends and I had peered in almost daily on the walk home from school but the store was piled high with mysterious goods so that we couldn't distinguish any one object clearly.

A suitable trunk was found and Dad stencilled my name in white paint on the sides of the trunk. Mom and I packed enough toiletries and clothing to last for weeks, although I would be home at the weekend.

I hadn't realised at the time that this trunk would follow me around Birmingham. The letter explained we had to 'live in' - live in the nurses home for one year during which time we would work in The Queen Elizabeth Hospital, Birmingham Children's Hospital in Ladywood and the General Hospital in Steelhouse Lane. Later in my training I would work in The Women's Hospital and the Nerve Hospital, but more of that later.

Preliminary Training School (PTS) was situated in two large houses, Priorsfield (now belonging to the University of Birmingham) and Southfield, both on Edgbaston Park Road. Impressed with these imposing properties, Dad stayed outside whilst a very elegant nurse tutor in a green uniform showed us up to the room I was to share with three other students.

Then came the bombshell!

"Don't let your dad see this! You can't sleep here! Oh my God 'Lizabeth".

Mom had been very quiet during the journey but was very definite about the fate of her daughter. The large sunny room was spotlessly clean but sparsely furnished: four hospital beds, two dressing tables, a linoleum floor with a rug by the side of each bed. The toilets and bathroom were down the corridor. I was so excited, I would have slept in a garret, but had to admit Mom was right, it did look very bleak. I reassured Mom I'd be ok and that I'd be home at the week-end, hugged and kissed her and Dad goodbye, keen to start my new life.

Girls of all ages, parents and porters with our trunks popped out of bedroom doors, blocking the maze of corridors.

I managed to find the room I had been allocated and started to unpack my leather document case (a leaving present from my office colleagues), new pens, notebooks and file paper, cosmetics and hair lacquer. In the 60s' hair lacquer was bought in a sachet of noxious liquid, which we dispensed into plastic spray bottles. The resulting spray set our hair like cement, often causing minor injuries to anyone foolish enough to get too close. I handled it with care as I knew from my practice runs that I would need a good few sprays to keep my long, thick hair in the requisite tidy pony tail worn high on the head so that hair did not touch the collar. We were not allowed to let tendrils of hair escape.

Later in my career a ward sister gave me a real dressing down because my cap was crooked. The fact that I'd just been assisting my colleagues with a patient having an epileptic fit didn't make any difference to her reprimand. As I mused about how smart and efficient I would be in my uniform with tidy hair, three other girls were shown into the room; they were to share my sleeping and dressing for three months during our stay in PTS. Although one disappeared after the third week, the remaining two became my closest friends.

The first few days were a whirlwind of preparation for the big day when we would visit our ward for the first time. We were measured for our yellow and white check dresses. All had been worn before, thin as tea-bag fabric, fitted us badly and worst of all were too long which in the day of the mini skirt made us feel and look ancient.

The following week, Aneeka bought her sewing machine from home and set about making us look a bit more feminine. The rule that the hem of our dress should touch the floor when we kneeled down proved to be quite a challenge. Aneeka sewed as high as she could whilst we practiced letting our bodies sag and shorten as we kneeled for inspection.

Dinah, full of innocence asked why tutors were so strict on this dress code.

"Come and stand at the front" said Nurse Tutor.

Bright pink, Dinah did as requested.

"Now turn round."

Dinah did as requested.

"Bend over to reach forward."

Dinah did as requested

She joined in our laughter. Her suspenders and stocking tops were well on display.

"We don't want to set any men's hearts aflutter" smiled Nurse Tutor. "I rest my case."

"Mm, not too sure about that" muttered Lou. "Could be useful if it's the right man."

The school required us to wear flat shoes. A blushing shoe salesman arrived with an assortment of different sizes of the same style. Flat, lace up and sensible. I hadn't worn anything except stilettos since school and these were a real shock to the feet. We behaved like truculent teenagers as the fumbling salesman fitted us with the requisite lace up concrete torture boots. The stiff leather rubbed our heels, which we were told were friction burns.

We learnt our basic nursing skills during *the Practicals*. Tutors taught and we giggled as we gave bedpans to our mates, laid up basic dressing trolleys, made beds with people in them and learnt how to complete the essential patient documents. Lunch times were relaxed and friendships were made as most of us went outside for a ciggie break.

A very attractive anaesthetist taught us cardiopulmonary resuscitation. After using chalk on the board during the introduction, he asked for volunteers to demonstrate cardiac massage. My hand shot up and I spent the rest of the day flaunting his chalky hand print across the chest of my dark jumper. Ah! Simple pleasures!

Later May 1965
First Practical Ward Experience

At last came the big day, well half day, on the wards. Driven by coach to the QEH we arrived during afternoon visiting, Nurse Tutor leading her brood of chicks to their ward. Aneeka and I were allocated to the same ward. Nurse Tutor handed us over to the first qualified nurse she could find, and ushered her remaining brood to their wards.

"I'll give you a quick tour said Staff Nurse and then after visiting time you'll be able to help with the bedpan round" she said. Aneeka and I exchanged 'oh joy' glances. (PTS hadn't prepared us for this! A whole ward of ladies needing to wee at the same time). We followed her down the ward.

Two rows of patients in beds or sitting alongside their beds, seemed to go on for miles. Two visitors to each bed smiled as we went by. Most of the patients were animated and called "Hello nurse" to us, but some were lying still on their pillows, their visitors holding their hand. We passed two beds where the patients and visitors were laughing and joking together, although both the patients appeared blue as they struggled for breath.

The staff nurse explained this was congestive cardiac failure. Their lungs and whole body were filling up with fluid as their failing hearts could not pump strongly enough to keep the blood and plasma moving. They were nursed on Z shaped cardiac beds, so they sat upright whilst their legs were low on the bed frame. Small cannulae were inserted in the front of their legs, with tubes draining into glass demi-john bottles. These were Southey's tubes to drain the fluid (ascites) from their bodies.

They had been in hospital for weeks, so they and their visitors knew how to make the best use of visiting hours. Even though they were seriously ill, a party atmosphere prevailed around their beds.

Staff nurse led us through the main doors to show us the side wards, usually referred to as *outside*. These were used by patients who could get up to the bathrooms without any nursing help, or for seriously ill or dying patients needing one to one care.

"I'll just show you the linen cupboard and Sister's Office, and then I'll ring the bell for end of visiting time. And by the way my name is Gail; only use 'Staff Nurse' to the patients," she said. Sister was obviously engrossed in paperwork but gave us a cheery wave of welcome.

The linen room was vast with every item of linen we would ever need. The clean fragrant linen was delivered every day in a huge wicker basket and was carefully arranged on the shelves so that each item was easy to identify by nurses in a hurry. I expected this would become my job, as I was the junior nurse, but all the nurses liked to do the laundry, it was an opportunity for a chat, a few expletives to let off steam and quite often, a short nap behind the door.

"This is the sluice" said Gail pushing the wide, port-holed door open. Aneeka and I knew this would be our domain for most of the time. Practical nursing with real patients always involved fluids from one orifice or another being dumped in the sluice, to be sent to pathology or sluiced away when the mornings work was completed. Pans and bowls were labelled with paper towels over them, the patients name and dire warnings 'For Biochem. Do not remove!'

One wall was formed of a cupboard full of lotions, metal jugs, rubber tubing and funnels. It was capacious enough to hide in, as evidenced by a sneaky packet of Gold Leaf and matches tucked in a corner.

Three student nurses returned from tea. We pushed the massive bedpan warmer into the main ward. I don't think warmth made the process of balancing on a five-inch high metal wobble board easier for the patient. Indeed for some of the larger ladies it was a white-knuckle ride as they clutched the bed sheets in their efforts to stay on board.

Taking a deep breath, trying to look as if I knew what I was doing, using my best PTS practised technique the curtains were drawn, bedpan positioned, used and removed to leave the patient happy and me ecstatic.

Most of the ladies were on fluid charts. This meant all their drinks and output had to be carefully recorded. More experienced nurses were able to look at a bed-pan of urine and know exactly how much urine was in there, but of course Aneeka and I hadn't yet mastered this skill, so we went backwards and forwards to the sluice to measure each amount and record it on their fluid charts.

All our ladies were given a washbowl to wash their hands and when they were happy the trolley was pushed back into the sluice and a first year nurse, Aneeka and I set about cleaning up. The bedpan washer, a wall mounted contraption, looking like a metal pizza oven only took one pan at a time.

Depending on the contents we sluiced them with what looked like a short shower hose into a bidet shaped sluice, complete with pull chain or popped them into the washer. The wash programme took about three minutes, maybe more, depending on the water pressure. Getting the pans clean was a lengthy business culminating with the pans going into a huge stainless steel tank, where they were boiled for twenty minutes and then fished out with a pair of huge tongs, often still boiling hot as the demand for bedpans was great.

After bedpans came 'back round.' All patients on bed rest were turned onto their side; bottom inspected for redness and rubbed vigorously with the hospitals' current favourite skin lotion a mixture of methylated spirit and nut oil. Bizarre though this must sound today, it worked, whether it was the frequent observation of their skin as we changed their position, or the potion, who can say.

Patients were turned from side to side at least four hourly and we inspected their elbows, ankles and all bony prominences for signs of pressure. Prevention of pressure sores was taken very seriously. Any patient admitted with a broken area was included in the Matron's Daily Report, completed by the nurse in charge. It was unusual to acquire a pressure sore in hospital, but if this disgrace did happen, it was reported to Matron and vigorously investigated

Then staff nurse announced 'tea break' for the late shift, Aneeka and me. As we walked down the corridors and across the drive to Nuffield House, Staff Nurse's long cap was caught in the breeze. I thought she looked wonderful and set my heart firmly on acquiring a long cap.

And so the first half-day passed. Bedpans, bottoms, tea and a real sense of achievement. I had got to know, and helped real patients and hadn't damaged anything or anyone.

On return to Priorsfield, we ate our dinner in relative silence, exhausted and ready for sleep. Breakfast on Friday was just the opposite. We had taken time to reflect. We shared our experiences, voiced our concerns, and laughed at our mistakes.

One thing we all agreed on; we wanted a long cap, blue belt and silver buckle, insignia of a trained nurse. They looked magnificent, especially if the breeze caught the caps as we crossed to Nuffield House for lunch or dinner breaks.

Qualified nurses who had worked a year in their chosen hospital wore mauve dresses with a frilly long cap and were presented with the hospital badge.

There was usually one 'Mauve' on each ward regarded with awe and respect. Their solid knowledge base and years of experience gave them great confidence and they were fun to work with. Ward sisters wore green dresses with a long cap, reigning over their wards with a strict, kind and calm approach to the care of their patients.

The week ended with a short test: several sheets of questions, relating to anatomy, physiology, the dilution of liquids and scenarios of possible incidents during our time on the wards. Multiple-choice answers were unheard of so we spent the morning writing our answers, handing them in to our tutors on completion. We would receive our results when we returned from weekend leave.

First Whole Day On A Ward

Our test results were fine and so we continued our second week of training. The first whole day on the ward, started at 07.45 with 'report' in sisters office when the night staff recounted what had happened during their shift. Then followed allocation of duties for the day.

The first year nurse, on her second ward raised her eyebrows when she was given 'Feeds, charts, sluice. The second year nurse was requested to care for 'Temps. BPs and IVs.' Care of IVs was a very responsible job. We had to set the plastic control so that the correct number of drops were administered per minute to give the patient 500 millilitres in four hours, or as the doctor had prescribed. Dressings and medicine rounds were to be carried out by the senior nurses.

Together with the first year nurse we distributed breakfast from a trolley laden with cereals and toast. Staff nurse followed with a heated trolley containing the ingredients for a full breakfast. Except on Sundays when the hospital kitchen staff started work later. I remember ending night shifts, desperate for food myself, having to boil at least two-dozen eggs in a huge saucepan. I felt like throwing a chucky egg when patients complained the eggs were overcooked or too soft.

All the patients were encouraged to eat, with nursing staff helping those who could not feed themselves. Patients' intake of food and fluids was carefully monitored; poor eating and drinking recorded in the patient's nursing notes.

The Ward Sister was determined her patients should have the best possible care. This included a daily bath or bed bath for every patient. Two nurses on each side of the ward bed-bathed, accompanied walking patients and provided washbowls to those who were on bed rest. This took until lunchtime and sometimes beyond, but the keen sense of camaraderie helped us to get through the sheer hard work of lifting and moving patients. Hoists had not yet become available. Instead senior physiotherapists had taught us to lift and move patients correctly.

Bed baths carried on during dressings, giving medication, accompanying patients to other departments. The senior nurse always checked the request slip that the porter handed to her, ensured the nurse had the correct notes, and most importantly, cast her eye over the patient to make sure they were decently covered with dressing gown and blanket. Dignity maintained at all times.

After lunch we carried out bedpan round and then 'back round' again. Most patients enjoyed a nap before visiting time. This was short and strict. The senior nurse on duty opened the door to visitors, strictly two to each bed, welcoming those who had become familiar faces. She remained on the ward to answer patients and relatives queries.

Life Off The Wards

So the days rolled by. I got to know my roommates well. Except for the mysterious Moira. Three years older than us, and very sophisticated. Moira's dark hair was cut in a bob with a long thick fringe, the image of the models we saw in advertisements and magazines. Of course her make-up was dark and moody to match the black jeans, well cut shirts and black polo neck jumpers she lived in. Moira told us she lived with her sister in London, but was reticent about sharing more information.

Of course, the less we knew, the more Lou and I fantasised, imagining her entering Soho clubs, adding to the smoky atmosphere with her Black Russian cigarettes, lolling gently to Blues music. We longed for the day when she invited us to join her, but Moira went home after the third week and was never heard of again. Of course this added to our speculations but if the tutors knew what had happened they certainly weren't sharing any information.

There was little time for socialising, but of course most of us became stir crazy, desperate for male company. I had a steady boyfriend at home but a couple of pints of cider were very attractive. So, a large group of us, maybe ten or twelve descended on *the White Swan* otherwise known as *the Dirty Duck* at least twice a week.

This wasn't as easy as it sounds. We had to sign out in the wardens ledger, were only allowed out until ten o clock and our condition carefully monitored on return. Some of my friend had hardly had a drink before and were keen to make up for missed opportunities. We had to support them past the warden, telling her of the awful sprained ankle they had acquired during our *walk*. These magically healed by breakfast in the morning, but their pale faces and monosyllabic conversations gave credence to their *injury*.

Eight weeks of PTS continued. Fortunately Lou shared my interest in anatomy and physiology so we practised our newly acquired knowledge by exaggerating the effect on our cardio-vascular system throughout our daily activities: the effect on blood pressure when we got out of bed, when we bent down, we feigned dizzy spells, heart attacks and recited the treatment. The scenarios became so extreme, usually ending in a call to dial 222 for *the crash team*. We were in stitches whilst our roommates, raised their eyes heavenwards and prayed for patience, or for us to grow up, whichever came the quickest.

We enjoyed early and late shifts on our ward. Our duties remained 'feeds, charts, sluice' but I enjoyed the interaction with all the patients, encouraging the very ill to drink, cleaning their mouths with foam covered sticks and smearing glycerine on their tongues. Some patients were grumpy, even aggressive but the Ward sister and staff nurses were expert at dealing with them, knowing that underneath they were probably anxious and frightened.

Move to Nuffield House

After eight weeks living at PTS, the magical day arrived. We were moved to live at Nuffield House nurses home, right opposite the main entrance to the hospital. However this came with one hell of a surprise.

We knew we were a small group of students, slotted in to accommodate the large number of people applying for nurse training, but due to the increasing number of students there were insufficient bedrooms. We had to double up in bedrooms designed to home one occupant. There was a washbasin, but only one bureau, one wardrobe but at least each bed had a bedside table, our only private space.

Fortunately Lou and I were put together. We became like sisters, sharing every off duty moment as we started our new life. With five new yellow dresses and twelve starched white aprons. We looked and felt like real student nurses. However the sewing room had carefully measured so that the hems of our kit were 14 inches from the ground. I am five foot six; many of my friends were much the same height, so out came Aneeka's sewing machine again.

Our room was nearest the lifts and we soon became the first place for most of our set to take their shoes off, put their feet up and often fall asleep on whichever bed had sufficient space to lie down. There could be eight of us at a time, drinking coffee and tea made from the hot water tap.

Trips to *the Dirty Duck* and do's at the University and Medical School continued but getting back into Nuffield House was difficult. We had to sign out and be back for 10.00 or if we had a day off the following day a late pass was granted until 12.30. Nuffield House was locked after the late shift drifted across so following a night out we had to use the main hospital entrance, running the gauntlet of a power-crazed porter. If we were seconds late signing back in he would leer, look us up and down, especially our cleavage and ask for a kiss.

There was no way this was going to happen, a pen stabbed into the back of his hand distracted him sufficiently to give us time to run to the lower ground tunnel from hospital to nurses home. Lifts were also turned off at 10.30 so we had to walk up seven exhausting flights of stairs.

Proper Nursing

Previously we had been extra to the ward staff, simply shadowing a more experienced nurse but now continuing on our familiar ward we worked early and late shifts with one day each week back at PTS for lectures. Practical training took place on the wards. With a qualified nurse signing off competences in our *Record of Practical Instruction and Experience for the Certificate of General Nursing* (as required by the General Nursing Council for England and Wales).

At 07.45 the ward staff met in sister's office for report, an update on patients welfare, treatments and specific needs for that day. The patient's condition was always given after their name and age. I was relieved to see the other wards nurses keeping notes to refer to during our shift. It was believed that bed rest was essential for most medical conditions and patients were admitted the day before they were to have investigations such as cardiac angiograms, techniques that are carried out as day cases now.

Patient-centred care had not yet arrived and at the start of each shift the senior nurse would allocate our tasks for the shift. She would carry out medicine rounds which took most of the morning, then came IVs and dressings usually done by the second or third year nurses whilst the beginners got feeds, charts, sluice. This meant we had to encourage patients to drink, ensure their fluid balance charts were up to date and make egg-nog at lunch time to improve their appetite. Each drink had to be recorded on their fluid chart, together with urine and bowel movements. At the ends of our shift, all the fluid charts were collected from the end of the patient's bed and handed to the senior nurse for checking. Any discrepancy she found had to be rectified before we were allowed off duty.

Respect for the patient was paramount. Walking down the side wards one afternoon, I heard a fifth year medical student tell his colleagues he had to "examine the old biddy" in the main ward. Fortunately (for the patient, unfortunately for the young man), Ward Sister happened to overhear him. "Mr. Smith, one moment please, in my office, now." She turned on her heel, her long white cap perking up behind her. He followed, aware from her tone that he was in trouble. I can only imagine the conversation, but I am sure he was left in no doubt that no one was referred to as an 'old biddy' on her ward and indeed in the whole hospital.

The phrase 'in my office, now' became a very familiar phrase, used when ward sisters needed to discipline us medical students, doctors or anyone who needed 'sorting out.' Maintaining patient's comfort and dignity became indigenous to every one of our activities.

One patient has stayed in my mind since the first time I saw her. I was asked to help a more experienced nurse bathe and turn Grace, admitted into our care earlier that day. She had been nursed at home by a loving sister, who had become reluctant to change Grace's position as movement caused so much pain. As a result, massive pressure sores had developed on both of Grace's hips.

Her sister had been too ashamed of Grace's deteriorating condition to ask for help. She had been forced to request a home visit from their General Practitioner when the decay of Grace's sores became too severe to cope with at home.

Grace had rolled into the foetal position; her beautiful wavy grey hair was all I could see over the bedclothes. A bed cradle (a metal frame) placed over the patient's feet, as she could not bear even the touch of the bedclothes. Her arms and legs, just skin and bone contracted into her body. We spoke gently to her but she didn't move.

I had one of the biggest shocks of my life when we folded the bedclothes back. Grace had huge craters of bedsores on both hips. They were so deep I could see the tendons and bones of each hip. Fast asleep most of the time, she groaned in agony as we gently moved her stick like limbs to wash her. Grace had Rheumatoid Arthritis a frightening progressive disease with hardly any specific medication available other than analgesics to control the pain. At the time, no one realised how the disease causes severe fatigue and lethargy so that sufferers preferred to stay in bed rather than face a pain-ridden day.

Despite our best efforts, steroid and gold injections, even giving a general anaesthetic whilst surgeons cleaned her sores to aid healing, Grace died peacefully in her sleep.

There was more rushing around than usual when the consultant was due to 'do his round' with his team of doctors. All patients had to be in bed, making physical examination easy. Matron often made an unannounced appearance on the ward so every day we made sure everything was neat and tidy. Beds were made with exactly the same length of sheet folded over on each bed. Pillowcases must be turned so that the open end faced away from the door to give a neat appearance.

There were to be no student nurses in the main ward during his visit, which created major problems for patients on diuretics (water tablets) to encourage the body to pass out more fluid and relieve the pressure on the heart. I and other junior nurses peered through the glass portholes of the sluice room, knowing some of our patients would need us soon. We fantasised about how to get a bedpan to a patient without a member of the medical staff being disturbed. Tucking the bedpan under one arm whilst crawling commando style on one elbow was one fantastic solution.

My Second Ward

After one weeks holiday, most of which I spent sleeping, I was eager to start work on my new ward, anticipating the drama of surgical nursing and I wasn't disappointed.

Gleaming stainless steel trolleys with shiny black mattresses lined the walls around the operating theatre. I could smell the clean anaesthesia smell I remembered from my few visits to the surgical block.

Report in Sisters' office was in an unfamiliar language but by this time I had learnt to note down what I thought I heard (hems of starched aprons make very good note books). I then asked my colleagues what it meant later. Getting the patients' name and operation status was the most important thing.

Right - into battle. I wasn't surprised when my responsibilities were 'feeds, charts sluice' but as I was working in the main ward with my first male patients, I was expected to be more independent, having passed my first mentored ward experience.

Fastening a plastic disposable apron over my stiff white apron I made a start on the bottle round, the urinal carrier looked like a milk crate on its side with wheels and a long handle. Getting it out of the sluice was the first battle, a bit like trying to get a trolley out of a door whose aim was to hit you in the ankles as viciously as it could.

I expected the noise of heavy wooden doors on a crate of glass bottles would wake everyone but fortunately for me, the men continued to sleep. I learnt later that it was the routine for patients with painful wounds to have analgesic injections about 7 o'clock to relieve their pain, encourage them to move around in their bed, cough to clear their chest and eat a light breakfast. I donned my plastic gloves and approached my first patient, described in sister's report as one of the three 'cabbages' (coronary artery bypass graft) that had returned to the ward after two nights on the Intensive Therapy Unit (ITU).

All three wore their pyjama tops open, showing the long wound where their sternum (breastbone) had been opened and pulled apart. This allowed the surgeons access to the failing heart which was repaired with blood vessel from the patient's own thigh, removing the possibility of rejection of the transplanted vessel. I knew metal sutures were used to close the chest and hold their sternum together until natural healing had taken place, but there was no way I wanted to wake these patients.

I wasn't too sure about the strength of their wired chest so approached the bed very cautiously, lifting the top bed clothes just enough to locate his urinal, remove it and replace with a clean one. Eventually urinals clean and sparkling, I tore the plastic apron off, washed my hands and joined my colleagues doing the breakfast round.

Eight of the men sat around a large table in the dayroom, watching TV as they ate; now wide awake and enjoying the camaraderie of their ward mates. They were all on top form when a new nurse joined the team. Some of these patients had been in hospital for a few days, preparing for major surgery; they shared ongoing jokes and cheeky comments. We joined in, aware that this bravado was to hide not only anxiety about pending surgery but also regret about their lifestyles. Smoking had taken its toll on their health. Major arteries in their legs had become too narrow to deliver the rich red blood needed. Some had had blood vessel grafts in their legs and used wheelchairs until the grafts had healed. Two men had below knee amputations to remove their gangrenous limbs.

I still wonder why anti-smoking campaigns don't publicise the loss of limbs to arterial disease as a consequence of heavy smoking.

After breakfast came the usual washes and bed making. There must have been something different about the waterproof fabric used to cover the bed mattresses; this was the first time I experienced burns on my legs. As we pulled the bottom sheet off the bed, static electricity made straight for our suspenders, resulting In small burn marks and an 'ouch' from me, much to the men's amusement, with many cheeky offers to 'rub it better.'

Most of the men made their own way to the bathrooms. I worked with Jennie a more senior nurse to distribute washbowls and a smaller bowl of hot water if they wanted a wet shave. Leaving them with the kit they needed, we drew the screens and left them to it for a short while. On return we soaped a flannel, held a towel over their groin while they washed 'down below.' Once this was accomplished, I changed the water and we rolled the patient onto his side to wash his back and bottom, dried well, then the same mix of nut oil and meths was applied vigorously to his backside.

During the morning theatre porters arrived with a slip of paper with details of the next patient for theatre. And then the words I had longed to hear; "Would you like to come with me to theatre? See how to handover?"

"Try and stop me," I thought as I helped prepare Henry for his below knee amputation.

Thankfully, the two-day pre-med (usually Librium) suppressed his anxiety and the surgical barber had shaved his legs and groin the night before. The surgical registrar had marked a large arrow on the leg to be removed. Naked beneath the theatre gown, long thick wool socks on each leg, paper cap on his head we checked his wrist band with name age and hospital number against the theatre request slip.

I helped transfer Henry to the theatre trolley, excited at the prospect of going to theatre, well at least into the anaesthetic room. As was the rule, nurses walked at the head of the trolley, notes and x-rays on the end of the bed with the porter pulling the trolley. We put overshoes on and the theatre porter and anaesthetic nurse pulled the trolley into the anaesthetic room. Our joint responsibility was to ensure the correct patient had arrived for the correct operation, we checked the information with Henry (again) his notes, wristband and the theatre list. He would go to the ITU at least overnight whilst he recovered from his surgery.

So what could I say as we left him? 'Good luck' was totally inappropriate. Goodbye was equally scary I settled for 'See you back on the ward.' I was relieved to get out of the anaesthetic room, feeling it had all gone well, but regretting my inability to find the correct words to leave the patient before his mutilating surgery.

"You ok?" asked Jennie eyeing my pale face, I explained my concerns, my failure to give some comfort to Henry.

"It is difficult at times but the pre-med and the new faces in the anaesthetic room seem to distract patients so they don't really remember much. Come on let's make up the bed for Henry's return." We folded his bed linen into a theatre pack, so called because the sheets and bedspread were folded so that It was very quick and easy to cover the patient on their return. Henry's bed would remain empty until he was well enough to return. Only very rarely did a day case occupy another patients bed.

That evening my mates and I discussed the appropriate words to say when we left a patient in the anaesthetic room. Lou and Dinah had worked on surgical wards so were keen to offer advice. Lou described saying 'Good luck' to the first patient she took to theatre, only to get an appalled look from the anaesthetic nurse and a lecture from the accompanying experienced nurse. Dinah had actually received a very gruff "I don't believe in luck. Look where I am now" from her patient when she said exactly the same. So 'Good luck' was definitely not the phrase to use. 'Goodbye' was equally scary. After much discussion we all settled for 'See you back on the ward.'

Spring 1966. Birmingham Children's Hospital

The first three months of the second year of our training were spent at the world famous Birmingham Children's Hospital. This was great; we were in walking distance of the pubs and the only two nightclubs that we knew. *The Rum Runner* was like home to us with Spencer Davis singing there regularly.

Our storage chests had been moved from the QE and placed in our allocated single bedroom. I was to work on the Orthopaedic ward. At 07.45 On my first day I presented myself at sister's office for 'report.' The only two chairs in the office were occupied so I joined the two student nurses standing for the longest hand over on record.

Children were diagnosed with syndromes I'd never heard of. Five cots in a room leading off the main ward were used for children who were not yet big enough for surgery. Nowadays babies receive heart surgery in the womb, but in 1966 they had to grow, most to survive their first year. A staff nurse or third year student cared for them, but occasionally I was asked to help.

I will never forget the parent's anxiety as we handled their very small babies or toddlers. We could hold a baby in one hand, they looked like wizened gnomes, ghost like with ashen faces, grey fingers and toes, blue lips and very sleepy.

Four toddlers were suspended on 'Gallows Traction', so called because babies 'hung' from a device to correct the hip joint of those born with Congenital Dislocation of the Hip. The top of their thighbone was out of the hip socket. Adhesive bandages were wrapped around their legs and then attached to a cross bar which hoisted their legs into the air so that their body weight put traction on their hips, putting the thigh bone into the correct position.

Babies adapt very quickly and these babies were otherwise fit and well with huge appetites, contented and gurgly when fed. Mom's family and friends came in to care for their babies. Once the babies were washed and fed there was not much for the family to do, just sit on a hard chair, although many of them got to know each other and formed their own support group.

The crying started from both babies and the adults when they had to leave to pick up older siblings from school. The babies twisted and turned their bandaged legs clinging to their mothers .We did our best but were poor substitutes for Mum. However a tiny piece of chocolate worked wonders. Obviously I kept a careful eye on them in case they couldn't swallow properly in their precarious position. Of course they did, their smiles returned and their arms reached up for a cuddle.

After three day shifts and two late shifts came night duty. I was anxious during the day; my patients were so tiny, but it was doubly worse on nights. Parents were not encouraged to stay so the toddlers cried for their moms. Crying is contagious in children and soon most of them were howling, red-faced hanging on to the bars of their cots like little angry prisoners. Having been told not to fuss the babies and having many jobs to do, I tried to ignore them.

I went to the end of the ward where a group of young boys with spina- bifida gathered in front of the almost silent TV. They were a cheeky group, encouraged by a ten-year-old to chat up the nurses. I loved their optimism and accepted the promise of a date when they recovered from their surgery.

At 11.45 on my first night the senior nurse had distributed most of the medication but left the liquid antibiotics on three children's bedside locker for me to give. They adhered to the 6,12,6,12 policy for antibiotics

I still have nightmares about Jacqui. Five years old, following a week of investigations and bed rest she was being prepped for heart surgery. A heart defect was diagnosed after her teacher noticed how breathless she became during PE and playtimes. When I asked why it had taken until she started school for her to be taken to the doctor, Staff nurse rolled her eyes. "Wait till you see mum. You'll have a long wait; she hasn't been in since Jacqui was admitted."

Jacqui was beautiful, like a little bird. Dark wavy hair, translucent skin with a touch of purple and a heart that could tire and stop at any minute and I had to wake her up to take medicine. How did I get myself into this?

I stood by her bed; convinced I was going to kill her with shock, very tempted to tip the liquid down the sink, even drink it myself. But no she must have it, as the risk of bugs setting up home in her heart was lethal. I touched her shoulder gently.

"Jacqui." No response.

A little firmer shake. Still no response.

Her tiny frame was curled into a ball, like a sleeping kitten. Then I remembered how I had given my kitten liquids when she was ill. I sat on the bed and gently cradled Jacqui with one arm, murmured her name and placed the plastic medicine pot against her lips. Instinct took over and she swallowed, nuzzled into me and went peacefully back to sleep. Tears coursed down my face. Must have been a bit of a cold coming.

Two more little pots of medicine, each taken easily by two sleepy hospitalised boys. I smiled; they looked like little angels now. These were the lads who had promised me a good time, their wheelchairs tucked away in the bathroom to keep a clear space so that we could access the bed to give any help they needed.

Staff nurse returned from dinner break, checked the medicines had been given and dismissed me off to dinner. Dinner time was quiet, none of my mates were on night duty and I didn't know any of the student children's nurses. I was glad of the opportunity to reflect on my little patients.

The rest of the night went smoothly. I never realised babies made so much noise in their sleep, not just little snuffles but loud grown up snores from even the tiniest baby.

I began to relax as most children woke early, early enough to take their 6 am medicines and then wash and dress themselves. The lads using wheelchairs whizzed around, spraying each other with water in the bathroom. I could hear their shrieks of delight, as I was busy changing babies' nappies.

My first rota settled into routine, I knew what was expected of me and got on with it. During the day when it was my turn to sleep like a baby, Jacqui was taken to theatre. We were told the op had been successful and she was now comfortable in the ITU. She was discharged home during my nights off, still fragile but getting stronger.

Lou worked on the baby unit where the under one-year-olds were cared for, each in their own little cubicle. Three nurses spent every shift trying to coax very ill 'failure to thrive' babies to take liquids from a bottle, a soul-destroying task, as it took days for them to become strong enough to stay awake during a feed. Lou was from a loving family and found it difficult to come to terms with the fact that many parents never visited their babies during their hospital stay and already she had witnessed two babies taken in to care when they were well enough to be discharged.

I must tell you about eleven year old Steven. A good example of how children become ill very quickly. Admitted from casualty he was unconscious with a very high fever and a small dressing on his calf. Playing outside with his pals a few days ago he had slipped and cut his leg. Mom had dealt with it very well but the small wound became red and inflamed so she made a doctor's appointment for Steven after school, but he collapsed when he reached home. Germs had got into his muscle and then into the bone, osteomyelits.

This was a killer disease until antibiotics came along. Steven's intravenous antibiotics dripped slowly into him but he remained very ill for two days. His parents never left his side, so we took it in turns to sit with Steven after finishing our shift, just to give them a chance to get some food and fresh air. Two anxious days later Steven began to improve. I couldn't help but think of and thank Alexander Fleming. Such a small wound would have killed this young boy.

I completed five rotas of nights at the children's hospital, each with memorable events.

Sometimes Mother Nature and adults can be very cruel.

Part II
SECOND YEAR TRAINING
GENERAL HOSPITAL
BIRMINGHAM

Early Autumn 1966

We returned from annual leave to start work at The General Hospital, Birmingham (GHB). Our trunks of belongings, mostly small saucepans, textbooks and, of course, the precious brown teapot, had been moved into the rooms allocated to us.

Mixed emotions is the best way to describe how we felt because I always enjoyed changing wards, so a change of hospitals was great for me and most of us were relieved to complete our placements at Birmingham Children's Hospital. We had found nursing children deeply moving and emotionally exhausting. We were full of admiration for the students in our group who had chosen to complete the Registered Children's Nurse award. However, deep down, we had to admit to some apprehension about our new workplace. GHB was known for treating accidents and emergencies, so who knew what we were going to see.

Senior nursing staff had prepared us well for our first years' experience for nursing complicated and extensive surgical procedures at Queen Elizabeth Hospital. During report they had explained what to expect and how to care for chronically very ill medical and surgical patients who were often in hospital for weeks. We often became these patient's confidantes, especially during the night. Patients needed to talk about their fears of their illnesses and their families, so we felt we knew and understood them well.

Here, at the General many of the patients would be emergency admissions, unconscious, after work and road accidents and probably very ill.

However, it didn't take long for us to realise the advantages of living in Steelhouse Lane.

Right in the middle of the city centre.

It was a girl's dream come true.

Right opposite: the city's main police station.

A few yards to the left; the fire station

A little further on; Aston University

The main importance of our location was the shops; Lewis's, Rackham's and the Ceylon Tea Centre. This is where we congregated to share our exploits from the two weeks annual leave we had enjoyed.

Helen had hitched a lift back home to Derbyshire on the milk train from New Street Station.

'How on earth did you manage that?' we exclaimed.

'I have my ways' she smiled mysteriously.

Aneka had been potholing with her boyfriend.

Two girls had got engaged and were off to the jewellery quarter to buy gold chains to keep their diamond rings around their neck when on duty.

Lou, Dee and I retold our exploits in a caravan on the Warren Caravan Site near Abersoch and Phiewelli. We slept for about three days and then realised we were miles away from both towns. Recent time and motion studies had confirmed nurses walked approximately eight miles on each shift, so walking to town wasn't a problem but we weren't keen on the idea of walking along country roads in the dark. We were perfectly at home in Birmingham city centre, but there were no streetlights near the Warren Caravan Park. The stars were beautiful, but the sky and our surroundings were pitch black.

However, a solution was at hand. Early one morning Lou was returning to consciousness after a particularly deep sleep and as usual the first thing she did was check the weather (that is to say she looked out of the window - Mobile phones and their apps. were unknown in 1966) and we were hoping to catch the last of the autumn sun.

'Liz come and have a look at this.' Parked outside a nearby caravan was a green Mini.

By this time Dee was awake and joined us at the window.

'Oh, what a sweet little car 'she exclaimed. Ever the romantic.

'It's more than a little sweet car,' said Lou. 'It's Potential Transport!!' Ever the practical one.

'Depends on who it belongs to,' was my cautious reply, the result of many social gatherings where I'd been cornered by other guests, delighted to discuss their spots and rashes. 'Might be some old bods with nasty rashes. If anybody else asks me to *have a look at this, nurse,* I swear I'll hit them.'

We decided that we would keep watch and find out who owned the *sweet little car*.

One in the shower, one preparing breakfast and one keeping watch, we giggled at the similarity to a police stake out on Z cars.

We were delighted when we saw the three occupants of the caravan. Three young men. But how to gain their attention? We weren't looking for love, just a lift out in the evenings.

'The way to a man's heart and car, is through his stomach,' Dee declared. 'We need bacon.'

'Bacon?'

'Yes. I've never met anyone who could resist the smell of bacon cooking.'

Off we went to the caravan site shop.

Soon bacon was in the frying pan on the gas ring. Windows open wide. Dee wafted the aroma through the window.

It worked.

'Smells good,' said a male voice. 'What are you cooking?'

Lou gave a sharp intake of breath and knowing her so well I knew she was just about to mutter 'What does it smell like?' so I nudged her hard.

'Don't s'pose you've got any ketchup?' asked Dee, eyelashes aflutter.

And that was that.

We provided bacon sandwiches and they supplied the transport into one of the nearby pubs. I know six people in a Mini sounds a bit squashed but believe me it was not unusual in the '60's to squeeze far more than six people into a Mini.

Impressed with Dee's initiative, and our insistence that it was purely *a business arrangement* with no romantic involvement, our group filed back to the nurse's home. We needed to unpack and investigate our new home. We were pleasantly surprised. Although the hospital was old, the nurses' home was relatively new. The home was named *Musson House* after Dame Ellen Musson, DBE (1867-1960) She nursed in London Hospitals and at GHB. She became chair of the General Nursing Council (the organisation that designs and monitors nursing qualifications). She must have been very understanding of a young woman's living requirements. We had our own, spacious room with wash basin and large mirror. Lots of storage space. Showers, loo and bathrooms were just down the hall.

After inspecting our rooms, the next important task; to find the student nurses' notice board, displaying the wards we were to work on in our new surroundings.

I shrieked when I read my allocation - Casualty. Dee was off to a male medical ward, Anneka to diabetic unit and Lou was to work on male orthopaedic, but more of that later.

We met to go to lunch in the hospital refectory. Access to the main hospital from the nurse's home was a walk through a large, elegant conservatory furnished with comfy settees and armchairs. We didn't know at the time that we would spend quite a lot of our late evenings there. The rules about going out at night had not changed. We had to be back in the nurse's home by 10.30pm. After that the doors were locked and we had to return through the hospital and wait for night sister to let us in. We still had to *sign out* if we had a late pass. These precious passes were only issued by the warden if we had a late shift or a day off the next day. Of course, the inevitable happened and one memorable night, three of us realised we had all signed out in the same colleague's name. Night sister's face was a picture when she unlocked the doors for us, but she never said a word.

To walk to the refectory, there were a few steps down from the conservatory, a passage between two surgical wards and then the vast ground floor corridor. We passed a set of double doors signposted *Casualty*. A long, curved corridor led miles away from the main hospital, adding to the mystery of Casualty.

Ah well. I've always enjoyed a challenge!

Early Days On Cas

07.40 hours the following morning, I presented myself to the Senior (very senior) Sister in charge of the whole department. The first thing that hit me like a wall was the smell. Sweat, stale alcohol, antiseptics making the place smell sweeter and many smells I couldn't identify. I was to discover the source of all the smells later. There were four or five other sisters buzzing around in charge of the different areas of Casualty. Hoping for courage, I patted my blue epaulettes, insignia of second year of training.

The place seemed full of people as Senior Sister marched me off from her office to 'hand you over to staff nurse.' I trailed behind, feeling just I did when I was an eight-year-old child starting my new school in a Victorian school building.

'I'll show you round while it's quiet' said Maureen (soon to be known as Maur)

Quiet? It looked like Birmingham market on Saturdays to me. And it was only 8 'o clock.

However, this was my first day and Maureen was showing me through the waiting room for patients and their family and friends. Plastic chairs were arranged round the perimeter of this spacious area. There was nothing to distract those waiting for their relatives and friends, not even an information board, let alone a television.

Maureen introduced me to the four registration staff on duty. They smiled, said a brief hello, and continued to register people from the very long queue. They had to write everything by hand. We didn't have computers, printers, or even sticky labels of patient's details. All information was written laboriously by hand.

Maureen walked me round to Cas. Theatres where fifth year medical students were cleaning and suturing wounds. A staff nurse was bustling between the two of them, supplying more sterile supplies, sutures and needles.

We walked back through the waiting room to *Front Door*. This was the area where nurses tended to the walking wounded. This is the area I was to shadow staff nurse for my first morning in Cas.

It was the most public of treatment areas. We had to take dressings that had been applied by first aiders and ambulance men off patient's wounds, cover them lightly, ready for the junior doctors to see. Often this meant asking someone with oily hands (Birmingham is a very industrial city after all) to wash their hands with a well-known grease removing gel.

The procedure I came to hate was removing butter from a burn so that the doctors could see the full depth of the burn. We wiped the butter off really carefully and gently with wet cotton wool or swabs but it always hurt. The senior nursing staff had started a campaign to display leaflets and posters in doctor's surgeries and community centres, explaining that putting butter on a burn is the worst thing you can do. *Instead put the wound under a running cold tap then just cover with a clean hankie or tea towel.* In truth the heat in the burn melted the butter which reached high temperatures and burnt into the wound even more.

After examination of the wound the doctor examined the patient, recorded the exact details of the injury and wrote their medical requests. This usually required an x-ray to show any bone injury or foreign body in the wound. We wrapped a sterile towel loosely around their injuries and directed patients to x-ray.

Patients had to sit and wait (again) to be called into the X-ray room. Then after the radiographer had taken the X ray image the patient had another wait until the film came whooshing out of the developer, a larger version of today's passport and identification photo booths in every shopping centre. If the radiographer was satisfied with the detail of the film, patients would carry their x-rays back to *Front Door* where they hovered until a nurse spotted them and put the films onto a viewing box ready for the doctor to see as soon as he was free - yet another wait for the patient.

I soon learnt to ensure x-ray films were displayed the correct way around. I had received an icy glare from a doctor as he dramatically pulled an x-ray I had placed the wrong way round, off the viewing box. The film flapped and clattered, he tutted and with an elaborate flick of his wrist, turned it round. Staff nurse saw him and lifted her eyebrows, but no one said a word. We were still in the days of subservient student nurses, and indeed most female staff.

Patients with a fracture were directed to the plaster room where a very experienced plaster technician applied the requisite plaster to stabilise the broken limbs until they knit back together.

During weekends the nursing staff had to apply the plaster. Luckily a *back slab* was usually used for the first day or two, allowing any swelling to go down. This was simply a piece of plaster bandage held loosely in place by cotton bandages which sounds easy but timing was essential. The back slab had to be cut to fit the patients' limb. Only white plaster bandages were available. These had to be submerged in a large stainless-steel bowl of warm water until the air bubbles stopped bubbling out. We had to move quickly to apply the wet plaster and hold it in place with cotton bandages, using our hands to spread any plaster remaining on our hands to stiffen the cotton bandages.

After a few minutes the plaster was firm enough for a sling to be placed around the arm or a pair of crutches supplied. An instruction sheet given to the patient and job done!!

Sounds easy but if you imagine the mess two toddlers can make with a bucket of white plaster, that's how we, the plaster room and equipment usually ended up.

'Mmm, plastered again,' was my mates' usual comment, eyeing the plaster blobs on my uniform. Just you wait, I thought, your turn will come.

Maureen asked if I had seen the off-duty rota (why was it always *off duty* never just *duty* rota?)

She led me to a massive board nailed to the wall and there was the famous rolling rota for all staff. Qualified, permanent staff had their names against a line of shifts whilst I and my student colleagues were nurse A,B etc. it took a while to sort this display. It reminded me of the London underground maps.

Once I had made head and tail of this display I registered night duty for me in ten days' time when I returned from two days off.

I spent about two early shifts and one late shift on *Front Door*, learning the layout of the department as I directed patients to the many clinics that ran alongside Cas. Patient-centred care was not yet in place so unless they were on a trolley, patients had to move around the different treatment areas to receive injections and dressings.

The injection room led off *Front Door* with a row of chairs outside for patients to sit and wait (yes, another wait), until the nurses were ready for them. Two of us worked side by side to apply dressings, slings, and to prepare and administer the injection of anti-tetanus serum and Triplopen, a strong anti-biotic. A thick liquid, no matter how skilled the nurse, it hurt when given.

After a few days I spent the morning in this room with a staff nurse. 'Always remember, the bigger they are, the harder they fall' was the only bit of advice she gave me.

I nodded in what I hoped was a knowing way, wondering what on earth she was talking about.

'Oh, and if they refuse to take their trousers down it means they haven't got any underpants on.' No novelty there then. After one year's nursing I had seen men in every state of undress and every position and even chasing round the ward in their confusion, climbing over cot sides designed to keep them safely in bed.

Injections were given in the 'upper outer quadrant' of the buttocks, usually a nice fleshy part of the anatomy. Sure enough, we had men reluctant to loosen their trousers, Staff nurse had her own unique way of dealing with them

'For God's sake man, I've been cooped up in here for four hours, shoving needles into men's bums. One more isn't going to make much difference. Now bend over!' They always did.

We agreed we would take it in turns to give the injections, so when she was dealing with a patient my job was to prepare the needle and syringe ready for the next injection. One man fainted and a lady 'came over all queasy' at the mere sight of little bottles of liquid ready for injection, before I'd even prepared the needle and syringe.

I cannot remember any medication being in a pre-filled syringe. We had to put the needle on to the syringe, pierce the rubber seal and draw up the solution. Then, change the now blunted needle, a practice that is frowned upon today. Everything was checked by two nurses before being given.

I soon discovered the necessity to repeat everything the doctor had said to the patient and those who had accompanied them, to explain 'what happens next.' Patients were too anxious and confused to take much information on board first time around.

A seven -year-old came in attached to a cupboard door. He had been using his finger to pick the lock on the cupboard door, desperate to reach the biscuits his mother had locked away. His anxious mother had travelled into Steelhouse Lane on the bus, carrying the cupboard door. We felt more sorry for mom than the boy. He had twisted his finger into the lock, so it was going to be difficult to remove. Staff nurse explained he would have to wait for the next theatre list when the anaesthetist would give him a very light anaesthetic and we could remove the door from her son. Other patients and relatives couldn't help but smile at the very glum boy and his bored mother sitting in the waiting room clutching a cupboard door.

I recall the expletives a young lady had used when I had to cut the plethora of rings off her injured and rapidly swelling fingers after she had trapped her hand in a car door. Two fingers were hanging off and I had to cut the rings from the remaining two rapidly swelling bruised fingers. She chose to be as awkward as she could. using the usual questioning of my parenthood, my sexuality and many other profanities which I could have joined in. They were like an anthem to some Cas. patients accompanying every word they uttered. I had become accustomed to being sworn at and learnt to turn a deaf ear. But, that night, I'd had enough of noise, accusations and alcoholic breath all over me, so I took a deep breath, leaned in close and, with as much authority as I could muster, told her, 'If you don't stop shouting at me, I'll tell the doctor we've run out of local anaesthetic when she comes to tidy your hand up. Apparently, sewing fingers back on is extremely painful and can be quite a long job.'

Let's just say my whispered threat worked a treat, I've rarely seen a woman change so quickly. All the waiting patients heaved a sigh of relief.

I wondered afterward why I had threatened her so. She was in full view of waiting patients and I am sure it was because of her effect on them, both appalling language and belief I was really hurting her. I knew she would need a general anaesthetic when she sobered up to sew the fingers back on and then many months of out-patient care.

Thick cloudy plastic doors protected the entrance to Casualty. They were a great indicator of arrivals. They were the only public entrance into the department and used by everyone, walking wounded, patients for clinic and those brought in by ambulance crews. The doors slapped together with different sounds depending on the weather and who was using them. The plastic was rigid in the colder months but when it rained, they clanged together *slop slop*.

The sound from the doors was different when an ambulance crew was bringing a patient for treatment. There was a metallic whoosh as the trolley hit the doors and then the familiar slap as they closed behind the patient. We walked (never ran) to the patient when we heard this sound, hiding our anxiety as we were never sure what awaited us.

The doors opened onto *Rooms* where patients were transferred from ambulance trolleys to Cas. trolleys. These were state of the art with hydraulic height controls and oxygen cylinders already in place on the base. Working on *Rooms* was exciting and the responsibility great. A large room was dedicated to resuscitation, designed so that a doctor could stand at the head of the trolley and just reach out for suction, laryngoscopes, endo-tracheal tubes and whatever was needed. When *resus.* had been used we had to check and sign that all the equipment was replaced. Everything from a thermometer to breathing equipment had to be ready for the next use. Even the blankets had to be folded in such a way that the patient could be covered in one movement, dignity always maintained.

Senior sister appeared to glide around the department as if she was on castors. I'm certain she had eyes in the back of her head, each elbow and probably each buttock as well. I held her in high esteem and so did all her staff. We all knew exactly what was expected of us and she ensured we had the training to do our job with confidence and accuracy. She kept the doctors in their place and stood up for her nurses in front of staff and patients. She summoned the nurses, medical students, and junior doctors into her office for disciplining, so it was all done very privately. We learnt to avert our eyes if a colleague or a doctor came out of her office looking very subdued and sometimes in tears. Luckily it never happened to me.

Eventually I was trusted to work on *Rooms*, closely monitored by the qualified staff working there. Although my first job was not particularly exciting it marked a huge turning point in my career. It was the first time I had been alone with a patient in a room, rather than in a ward with screens dividing us from other activities around us. It felt as though this lady was my sole responsibility. I checked her name from the green information card and asked what had happened. She had fallen in New Street, sustaining deep gritty grazes on her hands and knees. I couldn't see any other injuries and she was perfectly lucid when telling me what had happened. I had to prepare her for the doctor's examination, so explained I would help her get undressed and put on a hospital gown. I took her jumper and cardigan off, folded them carefully and placed them on the bottom of the trolley. I prepared a gown and gently removed her vest, then, to my amusement another vest and then a vibrant tea rose-pink full-length corset, only to reveal yet another vest and identical tea rose pink corsets.

'I have to keep warm my dear' she explained. I really feel the cold.'

Indeed, she was very thin under all those layers.

The doctor arrived and I stayed with him. No male doctor was ever left alone with a female patient, especially if a physical examination was needed. The look on his face was priceless when he saw the pile of tea rose pink corsets and underwear piled on the bottom of the trolley. He carried out a thorough physical examination, checking for any signs of deeper injuries or fractures.

'It was just a tumble doctor,' said the elderly lady, later to be referred to as a 'tough old bird' by the doctor when he recounted the incident of the lady and all her corsets.

Cas. Theatre

Two small theatres were kept for *clean* procedures such as suturing, reducing fractures, dislocated shoulders and knees. There was a third theatre known as *the dirty theatre* used for dressing and treating patients with dirty or seriously infected wounds. Twice each day an anaesthetist was available to administer a light anaesthetic so their colleagues could carry out procedures painlessly.

I was to discover the third theatre was frequently used to treat vagrants, usually with leg ulcers or injuries which had been neglected. Most of the city vagrants were well known to the staff who greeted them by name. Later in my time on Cas. I was to be the *dirty nurse* that is the nurse who 'stands at the back' with a kidney dish (so called because of its shape. I never actually saw a kidney in one). I had to be ready to receive the dirty dressings from staff nurse as she removed them to find out the severity of the injury. On one very memorable occasion she was removing filthy rags from a vagrant's leg. Layer after layer was passed into my large kidney dish. The smell of rotting flesh was appalling, even though she had anticipated this and had insisted on us both wearing two masks. As we got nearer to the leg we realised the last couple of rags were moving. She looked at me and I returned her questioning eyes with 'Yes I'm ok.' A few weeks on Cas. had prepared me for anything. The last rags were removed to reveal maggots munching away at the ulcerated leg. We recovered our poise as she scrapped them off into my kidney dish.

Now this sounds absolutely dreadful, but the truth was even stranger. The maggots had eaten all the dead ulcerated tissue and left a very clean wound which the surgical trauma doctor told us would be very easy to graft and repair. Our patient had no other visitors on his body, he didn't need delousing, so he was transferred to a medical ward, a comfortable bed, given a bed bath and booked into the next available theatre list for skin grafts to his clean leg.

A friend on the ward assured me his leg was healing and he was very popular with nurses and other patients who shared their chocolates and biscuits with him. She also assured me that a place in a local hostel had been found for him.

I recounted this incident to Nurse Tutor during our next study day. She had nursed during the war and explained how it was common practice to put a plaster of Paris 'glove' over the dressings on an injured hand, allowing blood and infected material to soak through the plaster bandages. Flies would be attracted to the pong and lay their eggs. The hatched larvae only eat dead tissue so they would munch away on all the dead stuff, leaving a clean wound for repair and skin grafting.

Casualty Night Duty

Night duty soon came round again. The nights were as busy as day shifts, never boring and time went very quickly.

Some lads enjoyed a good fight on Friday or Saturday night and found themselves accompanied by a police officer to Cas. Some of these lads were under age, some only 12 years old. If their wounds were superficial, we cleaned and dressed their injuries. By this time, often the young boys were in tears. I was never really sure if they were tears of anger or fear. We phoned their parents to come and take them home, or the police officer escorted them to the police station. Many parents refused to come to the hospital, requesting us to *sort him out* as they could not do anything with him.

What to do? In the flash of a fist this young warrior was under the care of social services and blocking a room as a member of the security team or police officer took up residence outside the door.

We had a spate of domestic incidents. Partners and spouses argued. Kicks and punches were exchanged. Often the female retaliated by biting her loved one's ear lobe off. Often, when they had calmed down, she would drive him to Cas. with his ear cocooned in a tea towel with a bag of peas to keep it cool. He was put onto a trolley, to keep him in one place as much as anything but also just in case he had other injuries. Alcohol was usually involved and both shouted words which considerably added to my English vocabulary. Often the female would continue to verbally rant and abuse her man as he clutched his ear before falling asleep on the trolley.

During night duty I discovered one of the smells that mingled with a million other smells was the smell of smoke from people who had been caught in a housefire and the fire fighters who saved their lives. Patients with severe burns were taken to the specialist Burns Unit at the Accident Hospital on Bath Row. We received the less severely burned but still very ill patients. Hot burning smoke is deceptive. If breathed in, the heat burns and scars the lung tissue, reducing the lungs' ability to expand. The lungs never recover so, even if the patient makes it out of Cas. they have breathing problems for the rest of their life.

There were victims of domestic abuse, usually on late shift and night duty. One incident still stays in my memory. She was a small lady, very smartly dressed but had been badly beaten up by her husband. Security took the man into the waiting area where he sat with his head in his hands. 'I don't know why I did it. I didn't mean to hurt her; it just comes over me.'

I chaperoned whilst the duty doctor examined her. Every limb and most of her abdomen was covered in bruises, some recent ones and every colour of healing bruises sustained over a few weeks. She also had a black eye. I wheeled her into X-ray. She was silent throughout our short journey and long wait in the department.

The doctor confirmed she would not need a general anaesthetic, so I went off to make her a cup of tea. When I returned to her cubicle she was slumped over the side of the wheelchair. I called for help and we lifted her onto the trolley. Doctor examined her and asked me to fetch a staff nurse. She had to organise a bed to admit the lady for urgent neurological assessment. The doctor explained he thought she had a bleed in her brain from one of her beloved's blows. A very serious condition that would probably need surgery to save her life.

A female police officer arrived to take her statement. It seems his meal was cold when he got back from work, after a couple of jars with his mates. She was busy with one of the children who could not settle and could not warm his tea immediately; so he threw the plate against the wall - after a few weeks on Cas I wondered if there were many houses left without meals slammed against their walls - then he had slapped her to the floor and 'kicked her a bit.'

The police officer told me the patient probably would not want to press charges, because she was frightened of what he would do to her if she did.

Something in me changed that night. With very little physical effort he had put the mother of his children's life in danger; if she didn't die she might be disabled for life from her brain injury and would certainly experience great pain in her joints for the rest of her life.

I know and believe men and women should be equal but ordinary men will usually physically 'out punch' ordinary women, it's the way we are made.

One of my abiding memories is the great number of patients who had taken an overdose, usually paracetamol. If they had not taken sufficient tablets to render them unconscious we gave them a carefully measured dose of Ipecacuanha to drink, to induce vomiting. It was a common sight to see a patient sitting in one of the cubicles with a cardboard bowl in their hand. Those who were nearly unconscious had to have a gastric wash out. This involved passing a tube down the oesophagus into the stomach. A funnel was attached and warm water poured into the patient's stomach. Then the tube was lowered below the depth of the trolley and the water collected into a bucket. The patient was often restless during this procedure, and we often got wet.

I will never forget one female patient, who after her gastric washout looked at me with such an evil look and said 'some bastard always interferes and spoils it.' Not words I wanted to hear as I stood there with water dripping off my plastic apron into my shoes. I was impervious to verbal abuse by now and just thought 'I'll definitely wear the wellies next time.'

I remember the first time I accompanied a patient to male orthopaedic ward. The long Nightingale ward had a happy, relaxed atmosphere. I knew most of the guys were motor cyclists as I had accompanied many of them to this orthopaedic ward. Several young men with leg injuries flanked the entrance to the ward. Their legs suspended in a complicated set of ropes, weights and pulleys to keep their legs straight. They were in hospital for weeks and so became very bored. They whistled and called to me, so I gave them a wave and continued into the ward. This was Lou's ward and I knew she was on duty today, but where was she?

I heard someone calling; 'Can someone please get this guy off me?'

And there she was, pinned to the ground by a patient with a huge dressing on his head, on a mattress on the floor.

What the….?

The porter and I abandoned our trolley patient to persuade the man with the bandaged head to release Lou. He was extremely confused and staggered into the porter's arms.

'We have to nurse him on the floor' explained Lou. 'He keeps climbing over the cot sides and he's going to kill himself, he's so unsteady.'

'Can't you sedate him?' I asked.

'Don't be daft. He's got a head injury. We can't even give him paracetamol. It masks any deterioration or hopefully improvement in his condition.'

Does he ever rest or sleep?

'Occasionally, but he doesn't know night from day.'

I didn't know much about this patient's injuries, but Lou kept me up to date with his progress. I'm pleased to say he recovered enough to go home but then of course she lost touch with him as he became an outpatient.

Anneka worked on the diabetic unit. Here there were a small number of beds for newly diagnosed patients or those who were very unstable and had been admitted from Cas. following treatment for a hypoglycaemic attack (blood sugar too low) or the equally dangerous hyperglycaemic coma (when the body does not provide sufficient insulin. Anneka told us of patients being so thirsty that they drank the water out of a vase of flowers.

On a lighter note, although not for the patient's long-term health, were her tales of outpatient clinics. She was amazed by patients lack of understanding of their condition but also by their reluctance to learn more to help themselves. I remember her recounting how a diabetic lady used the bus journey home to lick the sugar off doughnuts as soon as she bought them as this made them healthier for her to eat when she reached home later.

Dee was enjoying her time on her first general surgery ward. Most patients were *cold cases*, that is booked for surgery. We were used to ward sisters having their own little eccentricities and routines, but we shrieked with laughter when we heard about this one. In addition to the routine shaving of the operation site (thankfully carried out on the men by the hospital surgical barber) Dee had to carry out an additional procedure on her patients. Using a pair of forceps with cotton wool swabs soaked in boiled water she had to remove the fluff and gunk from all the pre-op patients belly buttons. This is a very ticklish area and she described some of the weird comments that could be heard from behind the screens on her ward and the giggling from both the men and women.

'Couldn't the patients do it themselves?'

'No chance. Sister doesn't trust them to do it properly, so it must be done by the nurses. The first year nurses are on nights off, so I had to do it.

'Soon as the first years are back, they'll put you on nights.'

'I feel like a mole anyway after the last few months. I get up in the dark and go to bed in the dark.'

It was true. Since out first ward we had completed so many rotas of nine nights on duty with five nights off to recover. The first night off was after we had completed our shift at 8 o clock in the morning. Sometimes we returned to work only three or four day shifts before we were back on nights.

Gynaecology Ward

The next ward change took me to gynaecology. Here women had their prolapsed uteri sewn back into position or their diseased uteri and ovaries removed. Surgical patients were in hospital for ten days post op - they slept for the first few days and when they were feeling stronger became very bored. The banter became cheekier and cheekier as their stay continued. They loudly and freely gave advice about men to me and my colleagues, mostly telling us to avoid them. (It didn't work)

One group of patients who did not share in their jollity were the (usually young) women who had used a *back street* abortionist. Many sustained horrific injuries even needing bowel or bladder surgery to repair damage. One patient who was sixteen-years-old had to have her damaged bowel removed and a permanent colostomy made. So sad. They needed all the TLC (tender loving care) we could give.

We could see Loveday Street Maternity Hospital when we looked out of the gynae. ward windows. When Loveday was full, we had to take some of their patients. We weren't midwives and unfortunately the patients were not going to go into labour to deliver their babies. They were losing their babies with a miscarriage known medically as spontaneous abortion, always referred to as *miscarriage* when talking to the patient. Looking back, the care available was very poor.

We had to ensure the baby and placenta had been completely expelled, otherwise there is a risk of severe infection or prolonged bleeding. The gynaecologist would examine her the following day, to declare she was well enough to be discharged home to recover. All she received was an appointment to be seen in outpatients in a few days' time to check her physical health, but emotional support was not mentioned. Thank goodness for NHS and various charities available now to give the emotional support so badly needed.

Operating Theatres

During our second year we had to spend three months in the operating theatres. I enjoy a change and Lou had enjoyed her three months rotation very much, so I was looking forward to this new environment. Here at the General we had appendicectomies, cholecystectomies, gynae ops, hernias and of course lots of trauma and medical emergencies. I was going to love it!

Two colleagues and I presented ourselves to Theatre Sister who welcomed us and gave a little pep talk. She reminded us 'the operating theatre is all about keeping the patients' blood inside the patient', so we were not to be apprehensive about seeing blood (I'd already seen a fair bit of blood and brain in Cas. so this had never crossed my mind)

We changed from our yellow uniform and put on theatre's blue trousers and baggy tops soon to be known as scrubs. A blue fabric hat kept our hair in place and a large double layered fabric face mask covered half of our face. Finally, we had to find a pair of used clogs which roughly fitted us.

I clomped into Theatre One as directed. The operating list written on a white board informed me the operation in progress was a total hip replacement. I couldn't see much as, surgeon, scrub nurse and doctor were gathered around the patient. The anaesthetist was at the head end with a green screen separating her from the surgeons. I kept well back hoping no one would ask me to do anything as I hadn't got a clue what was expected of me. I kept close to the *runner* a more experienced nurse whose job was to support the scrub nurse, fetching any instruments or dressings she needed.

I looked around at this very new setting. There was a gleaming metal rack of hooks on which a lone blood-stained swab was hanging. I came to know that a routine check of the number of swabs used had to be made before the patients wound is closed. An important part of the runner's job was to record the number of swabs used throughout the procedure, ready to carefully check with the scrub nurse before the wound was closed. ensuring none of the swabs were left inside the patient.

I recognised some of the instruments in the *basic set* used to open the skin and muscle from work in Cas. theatres. Cautiously I looked at the surgical instruments on Scrub Nurse's additional large trolley. There was a saw, chisels and a drill, just like in my Dads toolbox.

The surgeons were chatting about a recent football match and I started to relax a little. It came as a bit of a shock when the head of the humerus pinged out of the hip joint, hit the wall and rolled under the operating table. Frozen to the spot I felt a huge blush spread across my face and neck as the surgeon looked at me and bellowed, 'Come on nursie. Pick the damned thing up so we can get it measured.'

I had to crawl on my hands and knees, between the doctors' legs to reach the shiny bone. I held it in my hand, a truly beautiful thing, glossy white and very smooth except where wear and tear had roughened and worn the bone away. But I did not know what to do with it. I knew I couldn't just lob it back into the operating area, as the jaunty journey across the scrupulously clean theatre floor meant it was no longer regarded as sterile. *I'll have to wash it or boil it up* I thought.

Then I saw the runner was trying to catch my attention. She whispered 'Get a bowl off the back table and fetch a litre of sterile water.'

It felt like hours as I searched for where they kept the bags of sterile fluid. I skidded back as fast as I could in my ungainly clogs and stood alongside the runner. The scrub nurse half turned and frantically waved a pair of long handled forceps at us. I went to take them but was abruptly stopped by the runner grabbing my arm,

'No, no she's sterile. Do it like this.'

She held the bowl with both hands and offered it up to scrub nurse. Scrub nurse stood on a small stool, enabling her to reach the operating table and her instruments. For a moment, her extra height, theatre gown and cap looked very elegant, and reminded me of a Greek goddess. with runner offering a bowl up to her. Using the forceps to hold the head of the humerus, runner instructed me to pour the sterile water over the bone, rinsing any microorganisms away. Scrub nurse turned round, holding a sterile kidney dish into which runner carefully placed the head of humerus. They did this so quickly and efficiently; the thought crossed my mind just how many similar procedures they must have done before.

Scrub nurse then used a pair of callipers to measure the bone, so that the correct size was selected. She checked it was ok with the surgeon and called out the size to runner. But runner was not there. She'd gone. Scrub nurse nodded to me and I, terrified, realised I was the only person who could help. Fortunately scrub nurse was aware this was my first day. Quietly, she whispered me through the procedure. I had to open the box and present it to her so that she could remove the shiny, sterile metal replacement humerus so that it could be hammered into the healthy end of the femur. When I say hammered, I mean hammered, the surgeon used a mallet.

I felt relieved when Scrub Nurse told me 'You did well there, excellent.'

Theatres were very quiet during weekends and night duty. Unless we had a Road Traffic Accident or emergency surgery from Casualty. We had to spend our time cleaning the instruments. I spent many Saturday mornings scrubbing stainless steel forceps and oiling the joints with a little brush and nut oil. Instruments were placed in stainless steel trays and sent to CSSD (central sterile supply department), a new department that was to take over all the boiling and autoclaving we had to carry out on the wards. Another weekend task was to whiten the dozens of clogs from surgeons and all the theatre staff.

If we were quiet on night duty, we slept on the theatre trolleys, like sardines, in the anaesthetic room.

I thought the future looked bright for me in theatres. Little did I know how I was going to fare in my last assessment in theatres.

Miserable Scrub Nurse Experience

As student nurses, we had to scrub for a simple operation. It was my last week in theatres when Sister told me I was to scrub for a D and C. This is dilatation and curettage, an operation to remove any products of conception that are left behind after a miscarried pregnancy. I was very excited as I scrubbed my hands at the stainless-steel sink. Iodine solution right up to my elbows. Then came the most mortifying experience of my life. I had to put on a pair of sterile gloves. A procedure I knew well. But I could not get them on. Whether my hands were too wet from all the scrubbing or sweaty with nerves, I don't know. I pulled at the wrist area but all it did was stretch; my fingers just would not slide gracefully into the gloves. So, imagine my mortification when I turned round to see the patient being wheeled out of theatre into the recovery room, leaving me standing there, gowned and gloved and useless. The operation was complete, and I hadn't even touched the instrument trolley or indeed the patient. I was so embarrassed by this that when my friends asked how I was getting on in theatres I told them I had decided I preferred my patients awake and chatting.

For the next few days, all the cases we had were complicated major surgery or extremely ill casualties. I had learnt my way around theatre storeroom and could work as runner. Sometimes the surgeons would invite me up to the table to observe what they were doing. I was fascinated by the layers of tissue under the skin. Everyone has a layer of fat, but the density varied from patient to patient. Underneath the fat is a layer of muscle. Sometimes it was difficult for the assistant surgeon, sometimes two, to insert the retractors to hold the layer of fat and muscle out of the surgeon's field of vision. The peritoneum is the next layer in the abdomen, once this was cut, we could see the patients' organs clearly. Once surgery was completed these layers of the patients' tissues were closed, with catgut thread, silk thread and sometimes the new technique of stappling the skin edges together. Each surgeon had their own preferred way of closure, although this was often designated to the assistant surgeon. Seeing an operation close up taught me about the *stitching up* that lies under the skin. I was able to explain to my patients why their wounds were sometimes more painful than the small skin wound suggested.

However, time was running out for me to complete my theatre experience. I was delighted when sister told me there was a suitable procedure for me to scrub for. I was not so pleased when I learned it was a surgical emergency. A patient in Cas. needed an appendicectomy. Staff nurse knew of the shambles I had made of the gynae op. and realised I was very apprehensive.

'Don't worry. I'll scrub as well' she whispered, 'just as backup.' This was meant to reassure me, but it stressed the importance and urgency of the operation so my anxiety levels were sky high.

After scrubbing up I made sure my hands were bone dry, slid my arms into the sterile gown and twirled round for runner to tie my gown. My hands were shaking as I put my gloves on, this time quickly and efficiently. I let my hand hover over each instrument and looked at stuff nurse for reassurance before handing it to the surgeon. I had been taught to place the instruments firmly into the surgeon's hands almost like a slap so that it was a definite movement. I assisted the surgeon to carry out the appendectomy successfully although he must have noticed my hand shaking as I held out a specimen pot to send the appendix to Histology. The number of used swabs was agreed, and the patient's wound closed.

To everyone' s great relief we had removed the swollen infected appendix without rupturing it, avoiding potential life-threatening peritonitis. Throughout the procedure staff nurse hovered quietly in the background ready to take over if there was any threat to the patient's life. I was very relieved when she could sign off my theatre experience, I really did prefer my patients awake and talking.

Part III
THIRD YEAR

Blue Dresses

We progressed into our third year at the General and changed our worn yellow dresses for blue, but still had the short crisply starched white cap. Third year students were known as *short cap blues*, a year closer to being a *long cap blue*, a qualified nurse.

Night Duty As Senior Nurse

Being a 'third year blue' meant more responsibility. Of course, most of the time that meant night duty. Often, we were the senior nurse on duty, responsible for two or three junior nurses and the whole ward of patients. It was customary at the General for the senior to sit at a desk in the main ward. The only light came from an angle poise lamp draped with a dark green theatre drape. We spent ages adding up the patient's intake and output charts, making sure they were adequately hydrated. Then came the four hourly charts. The day of operation was marked with a red cross and the following ten days numbered so that nurses and doctors could monitor the patient with a glance at the clip board at the end of the patient's bed.

One night, I arrived on duty to find the Ward Sister waiting for me. I remember the awful sinking feeling as she handed me a pile of temperature charts.

'Look at these' was all she said. They were from all the patients in the main ward where I had taken and recorded the 6 am temp. pulse and blood pressure. Imagine my horror when I looked closely at the sheets, I had recorded the findings in the 10.00 am column.

'Was it fatigue, or do you need to visit an optician?' asked Sister. I knew tiredness was not a condition recognised by ward sisters so muttered my apologies.

'What are you going to do about it?'

I promised I would make an appointment to see my mom's optician during nights off. I have worn glasses for close work ever since.

My next rotation was the private patient's ward. One ward for men and one for women, with a couple of individual side wards.

I remember this ward as being great fun. Most of the surgery was planned, but we also had surgical and medical emergencies, usually heart attacks. Because I was able to carry out more complicated procedures, I loved it. This was also very good experience in both surgery and medicine for when I returned home. I was engaged to be married and would have to find a job in the local hospital. Ideally, I would find a job in Casualty, but this surgical and medical experience would stand me in good stead for whatever vacancies became available.

The Women's Hospital

To widen our experience we then had to leave our beloved General Hospital. Unfortunately, our group was split up with ten of us, including Lou, Dee and myself, sent to the Women's Hospital in Showell Green Lane.

This was not really a happy experience for us, although one of my set did go back as staff nurse after we qualified. Looking back, it was probably not the hospital which was at fault. The weather was cold and wet. It took two bus rides from home to get to the hospital which meant we had to be up at 5 am to reach the hospital for a 7:30 start. We had to work two split shifts each week. This meant working until 1:30 pm, having the afternoon off and then returning to the wards for the evening shift, 4:30 pm until 9 pm. It was too far to go home so we did our best to sleep on the sofas and chairs in the nurses' sitting room. It didn't work.

I remember it so well. Amongst the women having routine surgery we nursed women who had massive wound cavities caused by vulval and vaginal cancer. We had to clean and pack these wounds. This procedure was carried out twice a day, usually after a dose of morphine to kill the pain. The hospice movement had not yet taken off and these women were in hospital for weeks. We got to know them well, admired and remember their stoicism and sometimes humour.

Outpatients Clinic At The Women's Hospital

However, there was a memorable and lighter side to my training. We had to work in an outpatient clinic. I was lucky enough to be assigned to the fertility clinic. I sat alongside Senior Staff Nurse as she questioned the infertile couple about their technique for making a baby. In just a few days I heard one couple describing how they clung together for long periods of time. (Enjoyable but ineffective.) Another couple were trying to conceive through the woman's belly button. I was so amazed to hear this in the '60's.

One of the first investigations for infertility is to obtain a sperm sample from the hopeful father. We didn't have a room with magazines etc. for the men to provide their specimen so this had to be done at home. In order to keep the sperm alive and mobile the little pot had to be kept warm during the journey from home to hospital. We instructed the women to bring the sperm sample tucked into their bra to keep it warm. I'm sure some of them thought this was part of the magic.

Another test was a post coital test where swabs were taken from the woman's vagina to make sure she was not killing her partner's sperm. One memorable lady attended clinic to have the last of three tests before a firm decision was made about her husband's sperm. Her previous two tests had been negative, all her husband's sperm having been destroyed. She was delighted when the consultant told her: 'You're a very lucky lady this time. This time, the sperm were very healthy and active', chances are you'll conceive this time.

'Oh good' she said. 'I'm glad I've got it right. My husband is away you see, so I got my brother-in-law to oblige.'

This was followed by a stunned silence, I averted my eyes, pressed my lips together, kept my head down and decided to tidy my examination trolley whilst the doctor took a deep breath and very slowly and carefully put his pen down. We knew we could not look at each other for fear of collapsing into tearful laughter.

This ignorance of fertility was commonplace. It was not unusual to have women splitting their contraceptive pill into two to share with their friends and neighbours. They were both surprised at the outcome.

Spring 1968: Third Year At QE

With a sense of relief, we returned home to the Queen Elizabeth Hospital, forever regarded as our 'mother hospital.'

Now we were well into our third year, looming over us was the State Final Examination for Registration as qualified nurses.

General Surgery Ward

Often, we were the senior nurse on late shift or night duty and I was delighted to be sent to the general surgery ward. The operations were mostly haemorrhoidectomies, abdominal surgery, hernia repairs for the men and sadly mastectomies for the women. The men were in the main ward, the women in the side wards. I spent most of my shifts working in the main ward which suited me, I enjoyed nursing men. Many of the procedures, such as rectal examinations by the doctors and then rectal washouts, or enemas administered by the nurses were difficult for the men to get used to - some were mortified. However, the sometimes raucous, comments from nearby patients helped them accept the inevitable. Their humour certainly kept me going.

General surgery was full of men with inguinal hernias (in their groin). There were various repair jobs, depending on the surgeon's preference. Whatever the procedure, the patient's scrotum became very swollen. To help support their swollen testicles the men were given a scrotal support. Now, this was the NHS in the '60's so supplies were pretty basic and came from the supplier not quite completed, the waist belt having to be attached to the webbing, testicle supporting sacks, a task which we designated to the men to keep them busy. One memorable afternoon, I had to accompany matron as she visited each patient on the ward, stopping for a brief chat. She asked one of the young men what he was making. His reply 'I'm making a bag for my valuables' made me smile but Matron's suggestion caused many men to disappear under their blankets.

She replied, 'If you ask Sister she'll lock them in a drawer for you.' I don't know how I managed to keep a straight face.

Another of the men's tasks if they had haemorrhoidectomy was to prepare the pads to wear whilst they were still bleeding and sore. We only had sanitary towels to offer them and these came with a gauze outer covering. They had to make the loops at the end to tie onto a belt which we made out of Tubigrip. Of course, men being men, they had to twirl in unison whilst singing a stripper's song.

This reminds me of an incident many years later when vasectomy was a popular procedure. Two guys came to visit their friend who was still very sleepy after the anaesthetic for his vasectomy. They placed two large grapes in his hand. His reaction when he woke up, but was still drowsy was heard all down the ward. Other patients and their visitors must have wondered what on earth we had done to this poor man.

Specialing Victor

Our two and a half years' experience made us 'very useful' (Assistant Matrons' words) so we were sent to especially busy wards throughout the hospital 'to help out.'

On night duty (as usual) I was sent to 'special' a patient on a cardiology ward. This meant I was to look after only one patient who was very ill, to frequently monitor and record his temperature, pulse, respiration, blood pressure and heart monitor readings.

Victor had the usual saline drip into a vein to keep him hydrated and give easy access to his blood supply should we need to resuscitate him. Supported on a mound of pillows, pale blue grey in colour, Victor was alert, but very anxious. During handover, staff nurse on the late shift had described him as 'being in heart failure' and waiting for cardiac angiogram. But now staff nurse was explaining Victor had a rare heart condition. His heart was very weak and could fail to pump completely. If his monitor showed any problem, I must be ready to thump him with a balled-up fist, over his heart. This sometimes starts the heart back into sinus rhythm (a steady heartbeat). If this didn't work, then I was to call for the cardiac resuscitation team. Thankfully this team of doctors and anesthetist were aware of the circumstances.

Victor was in a four bedded ward. The guy next to him was asleep but the two men opposite were taking great interest in all the activity, indeed they were both clutching their call bells ready to call for help should I need it. I introduced myself to them and Victor and recorded his vital signs. All went well for a few minutes and I was thinking about settling the other three patients, making sure they were comfortable for the night when the two watchful patients called, 'Nurse He's going off again.'

I rushed over and thumped Victor over his heart. Sure enough, he woke up and smiled. 'Thanks love.' He heaved a huge sigh, to take in plenty of oxygen. I did the same, looking over at the red crash trolley ready just outside the ward door. I wondered how long such a weak heart could survive.

We continued like this for about forty minutes, Victor clutching my hand, occasionally taking very loud noisy (stertorous) breaths to keep his body oxygenated.

When Staff Nurse arrived with the medicine trolley, I asked her what was going to happen, how long was this to continue. Victor was booked for a pacemaker, but the Cardiac Catheter Lab was in use, so we had to 'keep him going' for a while. Thankfully, after what felt like hours, the lab. was ready. The specialist nurse came for Victor, together with two porters to take our crash trolley with them to the cardiac lab. Staff nurse nodded for me to go with them, more to bring the crash trolley back to her ward than any other reason. I couldn't see much in the Cardiac Catheter Lab which was actually a two bedded side ward off one of the medical wards. . However, I was so stressed that I'm just not sure what was waiting for Victor. I do remember being very relieved to hand a patient over to another's care.

After successfully having his pacemaker inserted Victor returned to the four bedded ward. I hardly recognized him. He looked pink and healthy. I took him the usual very healing cup of tea and toast, made him comfortable on a mound of pillows. He fell into a deep sleep, the heart monitor keeping me well informed of his condition.

Victor remained on bed rest, as was the practice, for several days and then was 'allowed' to mobilise gently. I must admit I held my breath the first time I watched him walk to the bathroom. But he was fine. Returning to the ward after nights off, I learnt he had been discharged home, fully mobile and very happy. Re-reading this in 2022, I wonder if I dreamt it all. How could such a situation occur with today's technology? But there it is, a good example of how very far we have progressed.

Return To My First Ward

As useful' senior students' we were moved around the wards that were particularly 'heavy' and needed more pairs of hands. During this time, I went back to my very first ward at QEH. I was surprised at how different my working experience was as a more experienced member of the team. I discovered Sister referred to the PTS nurses as *the lambs* and protected them from potentially disturbing incidents and sights during their first week's experience. Now I was a fully-fledged member of the team I had to deal with all sorts of dressings, often horrific pressure sores when patients had been kept in bed by well-intentioned relatives, often in so much pain, they cried out when moved and so their relatives did not move them, not even from side to side.

I remember one lady who had who had some sort of infection on her lady parts and the only cure at the time was to paint the area with tincture of gentian violet and to leave the area exposed. My daily job was to apply the gentian violet and help her sit out of bed. Patients were not encouraged to dress in their daytime clothes, nighties and PJ's were worn. So, this lady sat alongside her bed with her nightie hitched up with very purple, almost luminous genitals. She choose to keep the screens drawn round her, and who can blame her. I collected magazines from other patients to help pass her lonely time. I explained to the other ladies it was ok to ask if she'd like a chat, give her fair warning so that she could cover herself with a towel, and pop their head through the screens and say hello. Confidentiality meant I could not share her condition with other patients and the sight of drawn screens seems to bring out an apprehensive reluctance to 'visit.' Everyone assumes the worst, even the patient dying. Fortunately, she was 'allowed' back into bed for afternoon visiting

Third Year On A Surgical Ward

I was pleased when I was sent to a surgical ward. I've always enjoyed surgery more than medical nursing. I spent two happy weeks on day duty, running up and down to theatre, and dressing some huge wounds on patients' chests and legs after arterial surgery. The surgeon's specialty was arterial surgery on arteries that had become bunged up from smoking or diabetes, hopefully to save the legs from amputation. Unfortunately, this came too late for some, and I became very adept at dressing and bandaging the stumps on amputated legs. The patients were routinely given a generous tot of whisky or rum twice each day to dilate their blood vessels. A group of long -term patients kept their midday alcohol until the 10 pm dose, drank them together and had a merry time holding wheelchair races up and down the ward. This was tolerated by Ward Sister and senior staff as a good way for them to let off steam.

Inevitably after two weeks on the ward I was to work on night duty as the senior nurse. I had successfully completed my administering medicine assessment so was able to do to give the patients their routine medication and antibiotics. The only drawback was because I wasn't qualified, I had to wait for night sister to arrive and check the poisons and drugs of addiction. On my first night she did not arrive till about 10:30. We administered the postop pain relief and night sedation without any problems. This was repeated in the morning.

Imagine my surprise and anxiety when in the morning, the phone rang during my handover to the day staff. Assistant matron wanted to see me when I came off duty. I felt my heart sink into my shoes.

I left the ward feeling so shaky I did not trust my legs to take me down the stairs, so I took the lift down (forbidden practice) to Ass. Mats office. Her secretary did not look at me, just glanced at my name badge and pointed silently to a chair.

After what felt like hours, Ass. Mat. opened her office door and waved me in. She crossed her hands together and leaned forward on her desk, a typical pose when about to deliver bad news. I will never forget her next words.

'We trusted you in your role as a senior student nurse, and I'm really disappointed in you.'

'What have I done wrong?'

Thinking my hopes of continuing into my fourth year if I successfully qualified the pending exam were looking slim, she went on 'I am informed the lights on your ward we're left on until after 10:30 pm. You are aware we have a policy of lights out at 10.

Flooded with relief that I hadn't polished off a patient or there had been a complaint about me I was able to breathe again. I knew it was useless to try and explain and I didn't want to get on the wrong side of Night Sister so I said the only thing I really could.

'I'm so sorry. I'll make sure it doesn't happen again.'

'I'm sure you will, nurse. You may go.'

I'm sure there was a slight flicker of a smile as she waved me to the door. I went to join my friends for breakfast, still shaking and pale. I told them what had happened, but they took it very lightly. I had been absolutely terrified but their reassurance to this 'Bad Nurse' eventually gave me my appetite back. I did not mention the incident to night sister.

We continued to meet up for tea after an early shift. But now it was in the hospital dining room. We had all moved out of the nurse's home to live in flats, most of them just off the main Hagley Road, one of the main roads into the city. We still talk about living away from the hospital, especially having to walk to work at weekends as it was too early for the buses to run. During snowy winters they did not run at all, so we had many cold journeys on foot.

One of my friends made us helpless with laughter. She was walking to the bus stop after a late shift at the General when a man came towards her, exposing himself. Her quick thinking really subdued him as she told him, 'No thanks, I don't smoke', and walked briskly on. She said she was too tired to make a fuss.

Dee had been sent to 'special' a renal patient on one of the surgical wards. We were very impressed when she told us the patient had a kidney transplant, still a new procedure at the time.

'What's it like,' we asked, imagining complicated procedures and recordings.

'Really boring' sighed Dee 'I've never taken blood pressure so many times. Every ten minutes!' We all sighed along with her. Blood pressure monitors had not yet come into everyday use on the wards. We had to put a cuff round the patient's arm, pump it tight and use a stethoscope to hear the heartbeat when the heart contracted and rested. There was no automated recording, everything had to be charted by hand. Looking back, this seems laborious, but we became skilled at hearing different sounds for various cardiovascular conditions.

One night, as I was preparing my intravenous drug infusions ready for night sister to check, a complete stranger appeared from the entrance to the ward, walking down the corridor towards the main ward. I was nervous. It must have been about 4.30 in the morning as one of my junior nurses was down at tea break and I knew the other was attending to a lady in a side ward. I'd never seen this person before so automatically challenged him.

'Just a minute,' holding onto the ward door as he put his hand out to push it open. 'May I help you'

He pushed open the ward doors and walked to the first bed.

'See that notice above the patients bed?'

Deciding it would be best to keep this intruder calm until I could call for help, I replied, 'Yes'

'What name do you see?

Light was slowly beginning to dawn as I told him, 'Professor Smith.'

'That's me and I'd just like to see the patient I operated on today.' In fact, they're all mine, so why don't you tell me about all of them?

I accompanied him round the main ward and the three side wards, informing him of his patients 'progress. Thank goodness they were all doing well.

As we completed our early morning, whispered ward round, he shook my hand.

'Well done young lady for challenging me. Nice to know the ladies and gentlemen are in good hands. Good night.'

All through this encounter I wondered if he was who he said he was. I had never heard of any senior doctor, let alone a professor visiting the ward in the middle of the night except in an emergency. Imagine my relief when Ward Sister was able to confirm it sounded like Professor Smith when I described him.

A few nights later, I was doing my rounds, as was the custom every hour just to make sure everyone was alright. I kept the torch low visiting every bedside. One of the patients admitted for surgery the next day was deep asleep, very deep asleep.

It was routine for patients to be admitted the day before their operation day and it was the anesthetists' routine to prescribe 'pre-med' tablets to help the patient relax and sleep before surgery. Probably the pre-op tranquilizers was my first thought, but something made me look again. Then I realized the floor was sticky. It was blood. I threw the bed clothes back to see blood soaking the mattress and dripping onto the floor. He had cut his wrists. There was only one course of action: call for help and deal with the bleeding. I called for my junior nurse to dial 222. I knew it wasn't a cardiac arrest, but I needed some medical help here quickly. The whole crash team arrived. I anticipated some sarcastic comments, but they were suitably impressed with the blood loss to acknowledge he was near death. The patient received a blood transfusion, his wounds were sutured in theatre. I hardly took my eyes off him during the two days he spent in hospital recovering. Psychiatric care was arranged, and he was sent home to recover.

I made one enormous faux par whilst on this surgical ward. Out shopping I was greeted by a former patient. He looked really pleased to see me and I racked my brains to think what surgical operation he'd had. At the time a common operation in men of his age was vagotomy and pyloroplasty, an operation to help patients with stomach ulcers. I racked my brains and decided that had been his operation.

The conversation went something like this; 'How are you? Everything working alright, no more pain and everything going down OK?'

The look on his face was priceless and I realised I'd made a tremendous mistake. Next day I went on shift early so that I could check the ward records to find out what surgery he'd had done. Imagine my horror when I read he had been admitted for circumcision. My questions couldn't have been more embarrassing. That taught me quite a lesson, and to this day, I admit straight away if I meet someone and can't remember where I know them from. A simple 'I know I've met you before, but I can't remember where' saves a lot of embarrassment.

I assumed I was to stay at the QE until State Finals. Then came an almighty blow! I learned the powers that be had decided I had insufficient psychiatric experience and I was to move to the Midland Nerve Hospital (MNH). All on my own - none of my set was moving there. I was angry and anxious. There were only three months to State Finals. How could I take a state exam in General Nursing when working with psychiatric patients?

As it happened it was a blessing in disguise.

The patients were mobile (too mobile in some instances) so the work was not heavy and physically tiring. It was the practice at *the Nerve* not to put student nurses on night duty.so I had lots of time to revise when off duty and I was able to meet up with my friends from QE and the General during the mornings before late shifts.

Many of our patients had obsessive compulsive conditions. I recall one young man taking four or five hours to get up in the morning - he had so many checks to carry out that on a bad day he still wasn't dressed at lunch time.

I had to sit with a middle-aged lady who had anorexia nervosa. She was nursed in a single room with the pipe from the washbasin draining into a bucket so that we could monitor if she was vomiting food back into the wash basin. I had to coax her to eat. Every mouthful took ages as she spread the food out on her plate and chased it round with her fork. I had to accompany her to the toilet and weigh her daily. Any infinitesimal weight gain was celebrated by her doctor and nurses, but she remained completely impassive, as if her treatment and achievements were happening to someone else.

I watched electro convulsive therapy and worked in outpatients where I had to prepare trolleys for basic neurological examination. This consisted of items to test all the senses: cotton wool for touch, (and needles if the poor patient had diminished sense of touch), smelling salts and tuning forks. Tuning forks were used to assess the patient's sensory response to vibration, usually near the knees but sometimes at the back of the ear which made some patients wince if they had developed especially acute hearing.

I didn't know at the time but all this preparation and chaperoning for neurological examination stood me in good stead when I was taking the practical State exam. The examiner asked me to name the twelve cranial nerves and how they could be tested. My colleagues and I had chanted the rhyming mnemonic for the cranial nerves as we prepared for the neuro Clinics. I hope the examiner was as surprised as I was pleased when I correctly recited them. Thank you *On Old Olympic Towering Tops A Finn and German Picked Some Hops*. The letters don't actually fit the name of some of the nerves, but it was sufficient to get me through one part of the exam.

We had to take our practical State examination away from our training hospital. I went with six others to Selly Oak Hospital. When we came out we used the red public telephone box on the corner of Raddle Barn Lane and Bristol Road to tell our families we had survived. I still point out the site of the red telephone box whenever my husband and I drive through the area. The red telephone box has gone now; there's just a small traffic island but it holds a special place in my heart.

The following day we were back to work as usual. Relieved the exams were over and waiting for our results. These were sent to our home address and I'm happy to say I passed, and so did all my friends. The hospital was notified on the same day, so we had to go to the sewing room to collect our long caps. At the end of the week, we were on holiday for one week. Most of us used this time to buy an ornamental belt buckle to wear on our navy-blue belts.

At last, we had the long cap to float in the wind and the shiny buckle to confirm our status. If we worked a fourth year for the group of hospitals, we were rewarded with a Queen Elizabeth School of Nursing Hospital Badge and progressed into mauve dresses for our fifth year.

I requested to return to Casualty as a Senior Staff Nurse and spent two years there before returning home and becoming Ward Sister on the Male Surgical Ward at Corbett Hospital. It had been a fascinating and life-enhancing training.

MESSAGES FROM FRIENDS

After self-publishing my memories of the first year of our training in the booklet 'My Story' I received many emails and letters from friends who shared those early months. They reminded me of incidents that happened and which I hadn't include in my text.

Here are some of them.

The medical wards at QEH are in a six-floor block with a wide corridor running between them. Four bedded wards ran along the corridor. Each ward had their own sluice at the end of the corridor, near the main wards. We often saw our friend working on the opposite side wards as we cared for our patients in the side wards. One incident I watched, almost in slow motion was my friend's (let's call her Marcia), solution to having her ward's bed pan trolley out of action for servicing. Marcia couldn't face the thought of taking just two bedpans at a time, out of the sluice, round the corner to the side wards where there were about ten ladies on bed rest. So, she decided to use a stainless-steel trolley to wheel the bedpans around the side wards. All went well on the outward journey and indeed on collection of the used bedpans but unfortunately, when returning to the sluice Marcia took the corner a little too sharply and very slowly, almost in slow motion six heavy bedpans slid off the trolley and skidded like sledges down the corridor, past the side wards. We were helpless with laughter as the stainless steel pans gathered momentum. I had to help, so I stopped two with my foot, finding it difficult to concentrate over the weird sight we must present. Two bedpans had sailed majestically past sister's office, as luck would have it, just as I retrieved one from the floor, the surgeon and his entourage trooped out of sisters office.

'No thank you nurse,' said our most senior surgeon acknowledging the bedpan in my hand. I'll be alright till I get home.'

'Thank you, sir,' was all I could think of to say. Red-faced with mirth, clutching an uncovered used bedpan in front of the registrar, houseman and several students. I walked sedately up to Marcia's sluice, helped her retrieve the bedpans and left her to clean the trolley. Every time we glimpsed each other down the corridor we bowled an invisible bedpan down the corridor.

The sluice played a big part in our training. Student and qualified nurses used it to let off steam, have a crafty cigarette or a good swear about the staff or difficult patients, also to have a good cry on occasions.

I had forgotten some pieces of equipment in the sluice which we all had frequent dealings with during our first year as very junior nurses such as the three day stool saves kept in metal cans on the sluice windowsill and the metallic bedpan and urinal washer, whose door dropped open every so often and sprayed everyone with water, hopefully on the second rinse cycle.

The four-hourly 'back round.' It was the practice in all the United Birmingham Hospitals to inspect patients pressure areas every four hours, even during the night if a patient was especially vulnerable. Two nurses wheeled a trolley laden with a nut oil and meths mixture, talc and supplies to keep patients clean. We rubbed heels, buttocks and shoulders with the oil mixture to keep the blood supply flowing. We have known patients have sore areas on their ears and back of their head when they had been nursed elsewhere.

Many friends wrote to remind me about sterilising the instruments and packing the drums. Before CSSD (Central Sterile Supply Department) was established the nursing staff were responsible for cleaning and sterilising all the dressing instruments we used throughout the day. We did not have autoclaves, just a stainless-steel sterilizer full of boiling water. Prepacked sterile needles and syringes were available for injections, except the very fine needles and glass syringes used for giving insulin. They were carefully wrapped in gauze for sterilization. Everything was boiled for twenty minutes and then a long pair of forceps was used to remove the sterile equipment. These forceps were kept alongside the sterilizer in a strong sterilizing solution. This was fine, quite an enjoyable job. However, it had to be carried out at night. It was usually about three o clock in the morning before all our other duties were complete and so most of the patients were fast asleep. Imagine transferring stainless steel equipment (some very tiny) into a stainless steel kidney dish which you'd previously chased around the sterilizer in order to get a grip upon it. This was an impossible task to carry out quietly, causing many complaints from patients about the accidental noise.

Hand in hand with the sterilising was packing the drums. These were the size a of a Christmas biscuit tin, stainless steel and sat on the dressing trolley during the daily round of dressing patient's wounds. Filled with cotton balls, gauze squares and various sizes of cotton wool rolls. We would put rolls of cotton wool onto the radiators in the corridors so that the heat would' fluff them up' and give greater absorbency. This was a reasonably quiet procedure and usually worked well, until one of the new recruits on my ward decided to fluff up the cotton wool on top of the boiling steriliser. The soggy mess was unsavable. She had to visit a few wards to beg, steal or borrow some cotton wool.

Many reminded me about the early morning routine at the end of a night shift. We had to make the beds of all the patients who were 'up' for the day. This meant they all had to be washed, either independently in the bathroom or given a wash bowl in bed. All the men had to be shaved. There may have been up to ten patients to get up, so we had to start early. The one thing we all learned on our first night duty was how to knock the bed to wake the patient and then declare ''Oh you're awake! Fancy a wash?'' They knew our workload and I can't remember anyone refusing, even though they did fall asleep again sitting on their chairs.

There were strict procedures for making beds. The top sheet of the bed had to be turned over a certain number of inches (this varied for different ward sisters). The opening on all the pillowcases had to face away from the ward door. Last job, kick the bed wheels, so they all faced the same way too.

Our rooms on the sixth floor were so cold. We weren't allowed any of our own electrical equipment (not even a hair dryer) so couldn't use a heater. We soon had a solution, two of us hired hairdryers from the warden, set them on high and wedged them between books on our bookcase. We were soon nice and cosy.

Making early morning instant coffee from the hot water tap.

There are however many memories and incidents with patients and colleagues that I do not wish to print. Some, even after all this time would cause distress to the patients, their family, relatives and indeed to me and those who nursed them but I still hope I've been able to give you the real 'flavour' of nursing in the '60's.

THANKS

I would like to thank all the nursing staff who trained us, my friends for laughter and support in troubled times and most of all the patients. We couldn't have done it without you

I would like to thank readers who sent me encouraging emails and all those who bought my first book.

Sincere thanks to Sue and Robbie Gazey for editing and publishing my first booklet which I self-published and I send my sincere thanks to those who displayed and sold ; for me Julian Hill, my optician, Indie, our pharmacist in Oldswinford and Paula, my hairdresser. Many people contacted me, and I posted copies around the world. With their help I raised £1,000 for Spinal Injuries Research and Spinal Injuries Association.

Finally I am indebted to Oldswinford Writing Group for inspiring and encouraging me to keep writing. Special thanks to Lee Benson for his practical support and to Andrew Sparke for publishing this book.

MEMOIRS & BIOGRAPHIES FROM APS BOOKS
(www.andrewsparke.com)

Printed in Great Britain
by Amazon

42691652R00046